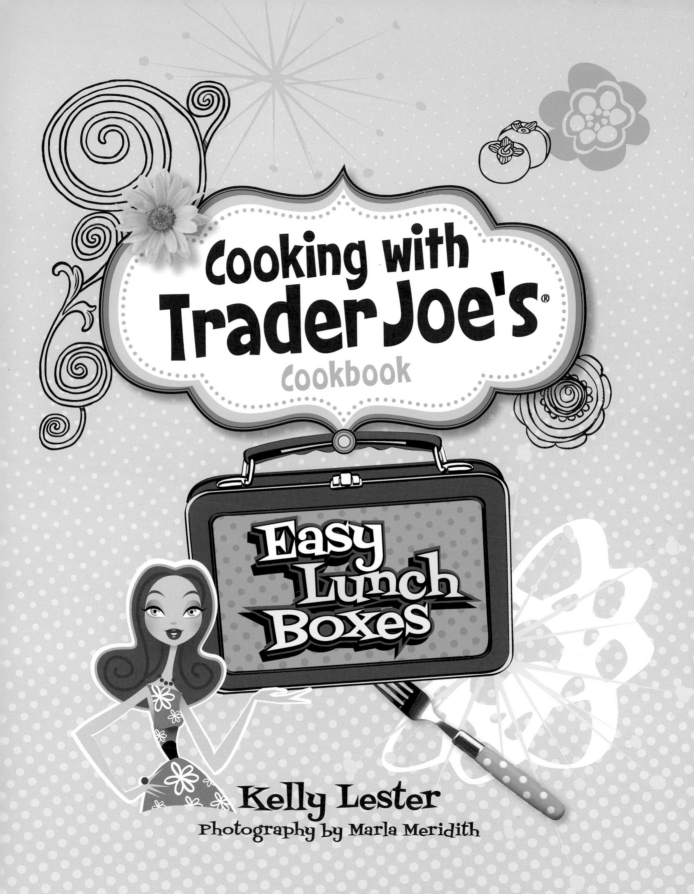

Cooking with Trader Joe's
Cookbook

Easy Lunch Boxes

Kelly Lester

Photography by Marla Meridith

Cooking with Trader Joe's Cookbook: Easy Lunch Boxes
by Kelly Lester
Photographs by Marla Meridith
Designed by Lilla Hangay
Produced by Deana Gunn and Wona Miniati

Published by Brown Bag Publishers, LLC
P.O. Box 235065
Encinitas, CA 92023
info@cookTJ.com

Printed in China through Overseas Printing Corporation

Library of Congress Cataloging-in-Publication Data
Lester, Kelly
Cooking with Trader Joe's Cookbook: Easy Lunch Boxes/
by Kelly Lester; photographs by Marla Meridith – 1st ed.
Includes index.

I. Quick and easy cookery. 2. Trader Joe's (Store) I. Title.

ISBN   978-1-938706-00-4
1-9387060-0-5

This book is an independent work not sponsored by or affiliated with Trader Joe's. Trader Joe's is a registered trademark of Trader Joe's Company.

Dedication

This book is dedicated in loving memory to my wonderful grandparents, Sam and Jean Landess.

My grandfather "Papa" grew up poor and never made it past ninth grade, yet he ran a hugely profitable business, despite having no formal business training. He just figured it out as he went along, ultimately employing hundreds of people whom he treated like family.

My grandmother "Nana" was a loving, supportive, and thrifty homemaker. She was an especially health-conscious cook, even in the days when folks couldn't get enough of those white foods like bread, mayo, and shortening. Even after my grandparents were financially comfortable, Nana would find a creative use for every little scrap. Once, she proudly showed me how a rubber band kept her shoe on her foot nicely, despite a broken strap. She also had better posture than anyone I've known.

From these two, I've apparently inherited an incurable entrepreneurial streak, an ability to make something out of nothing, and an ingrained habit of keeping my shoulders back, even when I feel like caving in. I wish they were here for me to thank. Their simple life lessons have never gone out of style.

Table of Contents

Foreword

by Bettina Elias Siegel

I met Kelly Lester after starting my daily blog, The Lunch Tray (thelunchtray.com).

I was new at blogging and not, shall we say, the most tech-savvy person. Then, a few weeks after my site's launch, I got the nicest email from this complete stranger. She tactfully pointed out some technical glitches on my site, gave me the contact information of her own web guru, and just generally offered encouragement and support to a fellow food blogger. With that warm welcome to the virtual world, I knew I'd found a friend.

The Lunch Tray is dedicated to "kids and food, in school and out," which means it covers everything from school food reform to picky eaters, the latest in federal food policy to recipes for family dinner. One question that comes up often is, "What on earth do I put in that empty lunch box staring me in the face each morning?" As a mom of two school-aged kids, that's a question I ask myself most days, and I confess I don't always answer it in the most creative fashion.

And that's why I love everything Kelly is doing to make the packed lunch an easy and fun experience for both the packer and the eater. First, there's her ingenious EasyLunchbox System. Something about bento-style compartments inspires me to create lunches that are more varied and visually appealing than when I'm wrapping everything up individually (not to mention the fact that I'm also reducing environmental waste). Kelly's products are just one feature on her site, which is also chock full of lunch photos, packing tips, and recipe resources to inspire. It has everything a harried parent needs to bring new energy and creativity to the lunch-packing task.

As much as I'm a fan of Kelly's, I'm equally a fan of Trader Joe's. I first discovered the store in Washington, D.C., and loved everything about the experience of shopping there, from the quirky signage to the Hawaiian shirts. Perhaps most importantly, the consistently great food products keep me a loyal customer. We then moved to Houston, and for years I've been biding my time, patiently waiting for the company to get around to opening a store here. Now I'm thrilled to report that Trader Joe's has just opened in our area – at last!

With the combination of Kelly's ingenuity, recipes from the EasyLunchboxes community, and Trader Joe's fabulous specialty foods, this book provides everything you need to create delicious, healthy and enticing meals-to-go.

Get packing, people!

Bettina Elias Siegel
The Lunch Tray

Bettina Elias Siegel is a lawyer and freelance writer. Siegel and/or her daily, widely read blog *The Lunch Tray* have been featured on *ABC World News with Diane Sawyer, The Today Show, NBC Nightly News, Anderson Cooper, the Washington Post, Bloomberg/BusinessWeek* and many other media outlets. She has also been published in newspapers such as the *Houston Chronicle* and the *Seattle Post-Intelligencer*, and in national magazines such as *SELF* and *Parents*.

Acknowledgements and Endless Gratitude

I'm big on thank-yous. First off, thank **YOU** for reading this! This book would never have come to be without the generous support of **my fans and followers**. I'm grateful for their non-stop stream of lunch-packing enthusiasm. They are creative, passionate, fun, and friendly. Thank you to **Wona Miniati** and **Deana Gunn**, who called me late on a Friday and gave me a book deal. Just like that. Amazing. Thank you to **Trader Joe's**, for being my favorite food store. Ever. Thank you to **Amazon.com**, the retail giant that really put this small biz owner on the map. To **Michael Agostino**, who pushed me to give Amazon a go, and who continues to push me onward and upward with his own special blend of sass and smarts. To **Sam Harris**, for saying yes to an old college buddy and for introducing me to Michael. To **Barry Williams**, my first lunch-box crush. To my brother **Lucas Richman**, whose musical genius created The Singing CEO. To **Wen Yan**, who deftly maneuvers things a world away. To my team at **Saddle Creek Logistics Services**, who deliver daily. To **Lilla Hangay** who made everything look so appealing. To **Heather World** for her clarity, insight, and eagle eye. To **Karen Ard**, who captured us with her camera and her warm heart. To **Raffi Zerounian**, for noticing the smallest details. To **Jill Dykes** for her attention-grabbing gusto. To **Glenn Rosenblum**, a manager and dear friend like no other. To **Bettina Elias Siegel**, for inspiring me to make a difference. To **Marla Meridith**, because a picture is worth a thousand words, but her pictures are worth a million. To **Lauri Fitzsimmons**, who dropped into my life like an angel and carried me through this project from start to finish. She was my right arm, my left arm, and part of both legs. She is the Queen of All Fabulousness. I cherish her friendship and so much more. Thank you (repeat that 32 times) to the **32 talented contributors** who have shared their recipes and their hearts on the pages of this book. To my brother **Howard Richman**, my favorite partner in crime, er, commerce. Without him, there would be no *EasyLunchboxes.com*. Thank you to my biggest fans: my wonderful and devoted parents, **Peter Mark** and **Helen Richman**, whose endless love and support got everything off the ground. Making my parents proud, seeing their smiles, has been worth all the effort. I just wish they would "get a Facebook" so they could follow along with what they started. At least I already know they "like" me. To my three beautiful and adoring daughters, **Jenny, Lily,** and **Julia**. Your future is the inspiration for just about everything I do. I hope you'll always think I'm the "best mommy in the world." And to my husband and best friend **Loren**. It's not always easy, but you always make it easier. You know I'd be lost without you, and this page is not long enough for me to count the ways. Oh, and to the **Academy of Motion Picture Arts and Sciences**, because this might be my only chance to thank them, so why not? I'm big on thank-yous.

About Kelly Lester

Over the last several years, some truly unexpected doors have opened for Kelly Lester, a singer and actress with over three decades of stage, film, and TV credits (kellylester.com). Kelly is also an entrepreneur with no formal business training. After her first daughter was born in 1992, she founded Art Plates, Inc., combining her love of graphics, collage, and home decor to make decorative switchplates and soaps featuring fine art. These handcrafted items were sold in hundreds of gift and museum stores across the country. Kelly sold that company in 2006. Three years later, she founded EasyLunchboxes.com, Inc., which was born out of Kelly's innate ability to do things efficiently while on a shoestring budget, and her desire to send her daughters to school with waste-free, healthy lunches.

As of this writing, her EasyLunchbox containers are the #1 best-selling lunch boxes on Amazon.com. On Facebook, she actively communicates directly with her fans, resulting in EasyLunchboxes being named a Top Ten Small Business Facebook Page by *SocialMediaExaminer.com*. Consequently, she has added "Social Media Expert" to her resume. Kelly is in demand as a public speaker, inspiring and motivating other entrepreneurs and small business owners with her story. Postings from her network of more than 20,000 Facebook fans were the foundation for this book of recipes, which suggests an overall recipe for healthy eating. She publicly promotes this philosophy and practices it at home with her husband, actor Loren Lester, and their three daughters, Jenny, Lily, and Julia, who all pack their own lunches.

About the EasyLunchbox System

Packed food can be fast, affordable, and green. The EasyLunchbox System makes it simple to organize and quickly pack meals without wasting money, time, paper, or plastic.

EasyLunchbox containers are a type of modern bento box. Centuries ago, the Japanese developed the practice of packing visually appealing meals in compartmentalized boxes. They called these meals "o-bento" or "bento." Traditionally, bento refers to a perfectly balanced meal with three parts carbs, one part protein, and two parts fruits and vegetables. However, another widely accepted meaning for the term bento is any packed meal in a box. As the creator of a bento-style lunch box, Kelly and her community of lunch-packers use the term bento in reference to this much looser definition, and that's why you'll see a wide variety of foods included in Kelly's containers.

Perfect for all ages, the BPA-free containers have three sections and easy-to-open lids. They're a favorite among families with young children, and folks with disabilities who may have a difficult time opening other types of containers. They fit perfectly into the colorful EasyLunchbox cooler bags with enough room for other items such as an ice pack, thermos, and water bottle. The custom cooler bag ensures that food is carried upright, not sideways.

EasyLunchboxes.com is a social media phenomenon. Going beyond tips for packing lunch, it has also become a hub for discussions about healthy eating. Visitors share everything from recipes to information about food allergies. The lively and often passionate discussions between Kelly and her EasyLunchbox fans via Facebook, Twitter, Pinterest, and YouTube, also cover family, home, and social issues.

Easy Lunch Boxes

Pack Lunches
Fast, green,
& healthy!

Introduction

Over the years, I've learned that the words "quick" and "easy" can send you in two very different directions when it comes to eating. At one end, you can eat fast food from a drive-thru or throw a bunch of pre-packaged, nutrient-poor convenience foods into a brown paper bag. At the other end, it's possible to create nutrient-rich, tasty and, dare I say, *fun* meals-to-go, quickly, leaving lots of time to enjoy other activities besides cooking.

The dinner bell

When I was growing up, my wonderful mother was not a big fan of cooking, to put it mildly. Preparing three meals a day for seven people (me, my four brothers, my father, and her) was not her idea of fun. She just wanted to get the food on the table and be done with it. During one stressful period, my mother was shuttling five children to five different schools, as well as to many after school activities, not to mention all that shopping for groceries, etc.

After all that driving and "slaving in the kitchen" (her words), she apparently had no energy left to walk through the house gathering us for the nightly meal. Instead, she would ring a loud cowbell, our signal to come to the table.

It's no wonder she preferred a fixed dinner menu that rarely varied from week to week: meatloaf, baked chicken, brisket, tuna casserole, fish sticks, fruit salad with cottage cheese and pecans, spaghetti (with bottled sauce), or grilled American cheese sandwiches with canned lentil soup.

Saturdays, when my parents usually went out, were Swanson TV Dinner Nights. (The only part I actually liked was the gooey apple cobbler.) Sundays were special: McDonald's Night. My dad would drive our Ford Country Squire Wagon to the Golden Arches and bring home their plain hamburgers. We made our bargain version of the Quarter Pounder by embellishing the buns with our own lettuce, tomatoes, pickles, and cheese.

My mother did have a specialty dish reserved just for guests: lasagna made with ricotta, Parmesan, and *Velveeta*. I had a happy childhood, but I can't say I saw much joy in cooking. So when I had three of my own children, I know I said – much too often – that I hated to cook.

My husband, on the other hand, grew up with a mother who worked full time, yet loved to spend hours preparing a fabulous meal. It's no wonder he loves to cook, and he's very good at it.

My family has always come first for me, but I also run a business and juggle that with my career as a performer. I just don't want to spend *hours* cooking. But hey, we all have to eat, right? So I've become pretty adept at finding ways to get it done well, and quickly. My streamlined method of putting delicious meals on the table is pretty much a combination of (no big revelation here) wholesome, fresh ingredients, and simple no-fuss recipes.

My old body and my new passion

People don't usually believe me when I tell them I've spent most of my life struggling with my weight. From the age of 15 until I was almost 30, I was overweight. I simply love food! I can still go through an entire chocolate cake in one sitting. But, as all of us compulsive eater types know, that cake is only enjoyable until the moment you realize it's completely gone [sigh].

I started taking better care of myself after I got married. I reduced my calorie intake, exercised often, and ate more fresh food, blah, blah, blah. Over the years, I slowly changed from a fat girl into "a fat girl trapped inside a thin body" – the battle to stop myself from eating the wrong things, or too much of the right things, has never really ended.

But today I'm in better shape than ever before, and my struggle has lessened, because I've developed a passion over the last several years for preparing and eating REAL FOOD.

REAL FOOD is food not altered to make it low in carbohydrates, low in calories, or low in fat. It's not processed with chemicals and additives. There are some who strictly eat REAL FOOD, locally grown and organic. I'm not quite there yet. My daughter Jenny tells me that I should eat only *vegan* REAL FOOD. She may be right, but for now I can't live without my plain Greek yogurt.

Basically, I eat whatever I want, but I do my best to avoid chemicals and additives, sugar and corn syrup, white flour, red meat, and partially hydrogenated vegetable oil... you know, the basic ingredients found in just about every meal in every drive-through restaurant and on just about every advertised boxed or packaged item at the supermarket. I eat reasonable portions and I don't snack. And I try to exercise at least a few days a week.

"A healthy body is a guest-chamber for the soul; a sick body is a prison." - Francis Bacon

Good reads

How did I get here? How do I prevent myself from devouring an entire chocolate cake while zoned out in front of (my guilty pleasure) reality TV? I read a lot. I love to learn what works and *why*. I've found inspiration in such books as *French Kids Eat Everything*, by Karen Le Billion.

She really summed it up for me in her fascinating illustration of the importance of eating REAL FOOD. People in France eat many things that we've been warned about: whole milk, butter, lots of cheese. Yet they're not fat. They have one of the lowest rates of heart disease in the world, and they are amongst the longest living humans found in any country.

It turns out that they form their eating habits as children. French children eat everything, including an abundance of fresh fruits and vegetables that cause food fights at many American family dinner tables. In this country, we cater to our littlest "picky" eaters. They get special children's meals at home and special children's menus at restaurants. In between meals, they're offered special, kid-friendly, additive-laden snack foods. The result? For the first time, American children will have more health problems and a shorter life expectancy than their parents. Childhood obesity has reached epidemic levels. We've all seen and read the news stories. It's a fact. I'm not being dramatic here when I say it's a tragedy.

An abundance of REAL FOOD doesn't exist in most schools. School lunches were gross when I was growing up, and my own kids won't go near them today. In addition to poor lunch offerings, many school children are also ingesting a steady stream of sugary treats, often used to celebrate a holiday, a classmate's birthday, or simply a correct answer to a math problem. What ever happened to the thrill of stickers, pencils, or (my childhood goal) a chance to be blackboard monitor?

While I offer products that simplify packing healthy lunches at home, I heartily support and have been inspired by crusaders who are working to make school food a healthy option, too. Thought-provoking, outspoken Bettina Elias Siegel works tirelessly to wake up parents, school administrators, and the government (local and national) to this important issue. She fervently writes on her blog, The Lunch Tray (TheLunchTray.com), how healthy food practices at home are being undermined. She bemoans the lack of control parents have over the foods their children are given during school hours.

Alas, since school food generally hasn't improved all that much over the decades (real change is SLOW!), the immediate solution that works for our family is packing our own lunches.

Problem Solved

I'm a "fixer" by nature – nothing drives me crazier, for example, than to find something around the house with a broken or missing part. Instead of buying a new one, I'll run to the store and, upon returning, announce proudly to my family, "I got the thingee for the thing" and they know exactly what I'm talking about. I might not have found an exact replacement for what I was looking for, but I found something that will work. So when I couldn't find something that would help me pack lunches fast, that was also inexpensive, reusable, and easy-to-clean, I had to come up with a solution myself.

Necessity was the inspiration for the EasyLunchbox System, which simplifies lunch packing, especially during those hectic mornings many of us are all too familiar with. My kids often hear me yelling a long word (don't worry, it's family-friendly!), and it goes something like this:

"Let'sgolet'sgolet'sgolet'sgolet'sgolet'sgooooo!!"

I'm proud to say that my EasyLunchboxes quickly became a hot-seller as positive word-of-mouth began to spread. I found that there were a lot of other people – especially moms who packed lunches for their kids and husbands – who were also searching for a better way. But then a completely unexpected thing happened: my website, Facebook page, Twitter, YouTube videos, and Pinterest boards became a hub for information about healthy eating – people share pictures of their packed lunches, exchange stories, tips, and triumphs, and make connections over conversations about all things related to food, lunch-packing, and a healthy lifestyle.

Write a cookbook - me?!

Enter Deana Gunn and Wona Miniati, the publishers of the *Cooking With Trader Joe's* cookbooks, who first discovered me on YouTube through the many videos I'd created for EasyLunchboxes.TV. When they approached me to write this book I knew they weren't looking for someone who hated to cook. There actually is a cookbook, first published when I was a kid, about "hating to cook" with recipes that involve covering everything in cans of condensed soup and sticks of butter.

Could I possibly contribute something new to the cookbook world? Deana and Wona thought so. They wanted me to create a book to show people that it's not hard to pack nutritious meals, *fast*. Oh! Well, I had that one figured out: you just need the right tools (check!) and the right food (double check!) My EasyLunchbox System makes it easy to transport all the yummy goodness that Trader Joe's has to offer. This book will show you how to eat healthy, even when you're away from home; at school, work, or on the road.

A world of real food lovers

I'm continually moved and inspired by the people I meet online through EasyLunchboxes.com. I read about families that are able to control or eliminate many food allergies and improve serious health issues by embracing REAL FOOD.

I love sharing their stories and pictures, the fun they're having creating themed lunches using little more than their imagination and a few colorful bento supplies. I've enjoyed seeing their tremendous creativity, ranging from hilarious to downright artistic.

I'm honored to share the pages of this book with 32 of these friends and supporters, all passionate foodies I met online, thanks to EasyLunchboxes. Their stories and recipes have warmed my heart as well as my kitchen. I hope we can all inspire you to join us in observing what I call…

THE THREE P's

1 PASSION. Learn to love making food as much as you love your children, your partner, or yourself. As this book illustrates, it doesn't take a lot of work or time, and we are all worth it.

2 PREPARATION. Make your own meals using as much REAL FOOD, fresh ingredients, and as few additives as possible. You don't even have to love cooking! Most of the recipes in this book won't take long to prepare, and some of the featured meals are quite simply "put together" from ready-to-eat food.

3 PORTION CONTROL. Don't overdo it. As my grandmother "Nana", who lived to be 93, used to say, "Everything in moderation."

I hope you enjoy using this book as much as I enjoyed putting it together.

But wait! There's more! If you love the meals on these pages, visit **easylunchboxes.com/trader-joes-book** for additional pics and yummy TJ's recipes online. I'd love for you to join us.

Enjoy your lunch!

Kelly Lester
Mom and CEO, EasyLunchboxes.com

A note from our photographer
Marla Meridith

When Kelly first asked me to take the photographs for this book, I was out in the crisp air, enjoying a high altitude family vacation. Her call caught me on a ski-bunny lunch break.

"A book? What? You're writing an EasyLunchboxes cookbook? Count me in, I'm your girl! Yes, I will contribute recipes, then cook, style and photograph 85 lunch boxes." Gulp. I finished my lunch and thought, "Oh my goodness. I just signed up for a SUPER huge task. And I love it!"

I have not always been a photographer. I started taking pictures of food about three years ago. With my iPhone. Since then, my photography has rapidly evolved, and now I have a big DSLR camera glued to my face at all times. Prior to photography, I worked in textile and graphic design. I live, eat, and breathe color and light. Composition comes naturally to me.

My kids can tell you how obsessed I am with photography. They are often my subjects (and not always willing participants) in many photo shoots. My iPhone comes out for quickie shots, but with my DSLR I now swap out lenses like a pro. I'm a natural light photographer, aka a "Light Chaser". Thankfully, the light moves as quickly as I do. I believe we eat with our eyes first. Food needs to look beautiful, edible, and inviting. I hover over food, finding its best angles, highlights, and disposition. I play it cheesy '80s music and ask it to dance for me. (For real.) I enjoy the thrill of capturing all different types of foods and then tying the images back into lifestyle and travel articles.

I hope you enjoy journeying through these lunch box meals as much as I had fun photographing them for you. I can tell you too: Each one is utterly irresistible and delicious. As the photographer and stylist, I also got to play recipe tester. Another great advantage to my job!

Pop on over to FamilyFreshCooking.com for recipes, fun lifestyle posts, crafts and more! For more eye candy, check out my photography portfolio at MarlaMeridith.com - *Marla*

About Trader Joe's

I don't know anyone who doesn't love Trader Joe's, do you? In fact, like me, a lot of people will say, "Oh, I'm obsessed with Trader Joe's!" I love this marvelous grocery store for a variety of reasons, not the least of which relates directly to this book: The food they sell doesn't have a lot of ingredients like artificial flavors, colors, or additives. When you compare the labels on Trader Joe's products to items found at other stores, you'll notice what's missing: a long list of chemicals, fillers, and preservatives.

Shopping here will save lots of time in the kitchen, too. You can fill your cart with everything you need to assemble quick meals, thanks to their fresh, ready-to-use ingredients, pre-washed and chopped veggies, pre-cooked dishes, and prepared sauces. Plus, they have something in just about every category of grocery, so it's truly one-stop shopping. Their food and wine choices are unique, and they have knowledgeable employees who clearly love their jobs. The staff tests all the food before they put it on the shelves. And they look awfully cute in those Hawaiian shirts.

About These Meals

Here's what you'll find

If you're looking for streamlined suggestions for packing quick and healthy meals-to-go, this book is for you.

Let's be realistic – most of us don't want to spend a lot of time making labor-intensive school lunches or complicated four-course meals to take to work. The effort we put into cooking intricate specialty dishes or recipes that require hours of prep work is most often reserved for family meals when we can enjoy lingering around the table with our loved ones.

Is packing good food quickly a high priority for you? Then you'll be happy to discover ways to do just that on the pages that follow. My delightful contributors and I have put together a collection of simple meals so you can get out the door in no time and get on with your day. Some require no more effort than opening a few packages of already prepared foods.

While many of the ingredients are generic, we've capitalized the names of unique Trader Joe's products, such as Fresh Bruschetta Sauce or Chunky Salsa throughout the recipes. It's not a requirement to get everything at Trader Joe's, but it's a convenience I invite you to embrace. If you don't have a Trader Joe's in your area, or an item is out of stock or (heaven forbid) discontinued, you can easily substitute most items with those found in other grocery stores. Check out the handy running list of substitutions on the publisher's website (cookTJ.com).

Nutritional information

Nearly all the detailed recipes included in this book have been evaluated by a team of certified dieticians and nutritionists. Nutritional data is given so you can match menus to your dietary needs. Unless otherwise specified, analysis assumes 1% milk, large eggs, low-fat yogurt, wheat bread, and low-sodium broth. Optional ingredients were not included in nutritional analysis. Although some chapters offer meals for specific dietary needs, you'll find that throughout the book we have also noted recipes that can be made vegetarian, vegan, and gluten-free by offering substitution suggestions.

Serving Sizes

When indicating serving sizes, we follow conventional measurements and guidelines in other cookbooks as well as the advice of our dieticians. However, in practice, serving sizes can vary widely. For example, my husband can easily eat twice as much your 9-year-old, so serving size is not a one-size-fits-all measure. If you're feeding hungry teenagers or throwing a party for the football team, allow for larger serving sizes.

For Severe Allergies

Persons with severe allergies (such as gluten or nuts) should note that unless a product is labeled and tested to be free of a specific allergen and produced in a dedicated facility, there is possibility of cross-contamination. In addition, package ingredients may change. Please always check ingredient labels carefully.

Pack it (Really) Fast!

When you're (really) crunched for time

Let's start off with the simplest, fastest way to pack a meal: Even though this is a cookbook, I'm going to give you permission here not to cook. So wait. What's up with the contradiction? Well, sometimes you just don't feel like cooking, and that's okay. You can still put together a great meal, even if the only effort you want to expend is to grab and go.

But hey, you're in a hurry. So after you get to know my fast-packing family, we'll share some of our favorite lunch ideas to get you out the door... fast!

Lesterworld

Lesterworld began on our first date, when I learned that "love at first sight" is not just in fairy tales. Loren and I talked for hours that first night. We're both actors who love working on the stage, and we both dreamed of moving to New York.

Just a few months later, we were engaged and living in the Big Apple. Our dreams now included how we would raise our children, and we agreed on one thing for sure: If we had a son, his name would be Sam, because we each had a beloved grandfather with that name. As fate would have it, we moved back to Los Angeles and had three daughters, Jenny, Lily, and Julia.

There's an old rule that comedy is funniest when it's "in threes." I can tell you that our three girls make us laugh. A lot. There's also something magical about "three sisters" in a family of actors. The concept has been explored by famous dramatists like Chekhov, Shakespeare, and even Woody Allen. With so many plays and screenplays featuring three sisters, it's no wonder, I guess, that all three of them love to perform. (It was also inevitable, I suppose, because acting as a profession goes back at least two generations in both our families.)

Lily: "You know you live in a house of performers when your mom is off rehearsing a musical in Hollywood, your older sister is in college studying musical theatre, your younger sister is taking dance classes all afternoon, you yourself are in two shows at the same time, and your father is reading his lines out loud for the next day's shoot :)......I love my family ♥ ♥ ♥ ♥ ♥."

I'm surrounded by a family that loves to act out in the kitchen. They each have specialties: Jenny cooks great vegetarian and vegan meals, Lily specializes in soups and stir fry, and Julia likes to make appetizers or entrées in tapas-size portions. Loren often recreates his mom's specialty dishes like matzo ball soup and turkey meatloaf. We all look forward to the breakfasts he whips up on the weekend. And me? I'll happily eat any meal that I don't have to cook myself.

We watch a lot of TV together (we like to call it "research"), but then again, Loren and I grew up watching a LOT of TV and we turned out OK. Being a serial multi-tasker, I combine my important activities whenever possible. To keep in shape, I use a cross-trainer machine (parked in front of the TV, natch), I walk while listening to business-training podcasts on my iPhone, or I pedal an exercise bike which is outfitted with a mini-desk (I'm not kidding) so I can work on my laptop at the same time. More multi-tasking madness.

Even though I spend most days parked in front of my computer, running EasyLunchboxes from our den, at least my girls know exactly where to find me when they need to talk. I'm proud of the fact that I can be there for them, even though I never seem to stop working.

Julia: "I love to cook. I chase everyone out of the kitchen so it will be a big surprise."

Jenny: "Going away to college in another state – and being completely on my own – quickly made me realize how independent a person I am, and how much of that is thanks to my mom. It also became very clear to me that she was totally right about pretty much everything I fought her on during high school (sorry, Mom). She gets a phone call at least once a week where I say 'Oh my gosh, Mommy, you were sooooo right!' "

Loren: "Kelly is the rule-maker and I'm occasionally the rule-breaker (that's just part of my job as 'entertainment director' – goofing around, planning weekend activities and general fun), but we all agree that taking care of ourselves and eating healthy will give us the best chance to be a family together for a long, long time. Kelly and I were engaged after dating only a couple of months so I had no idea what I was *really* getting. I knew I was marrying a beautiful actress, singer, serial organizer, 'bargain shopper' and soul mate, but I had no idea that I was also marrying an entrepreneur, computer expert, mother-of-the-year (every year) and now...author. Lucky? Blessed? Yes and yes."

Lesterworld is full of surprises. It's an ongoing adventure, crazier and more wonderful than I could have imagined... and I'm honored to share a snapshot of our lives with you.

From our family to yours...

Five-Minute Mac & Cheese

It seems like every morning at my house, you hear the same dialogue: "Hurry up! ...You're gonna be late...get in the car...now!!" Lily lets the night get away from her when she's on Facebook and can't understand why she'll oversleep in the morning. After her alarm goes off, Julia can take a while choosing just the right fashion statement for the day. We have a rule that they have to pack their lunches the night before, but sometimes they forget. Add a morning emergency like a missing cellphone or dance leggings, and you'll have only a few minutes left to make lunch. This is a great kid's meal we can make in five minutes. Mac 'n cheese was not a finger food when I was growing up (at least not after age two) but TJ's has come up with an innovation. A variation on the fried cheese ball: the fried mac 'n' cheese ball. Combine it with a serving of fruit and vegetables, and in five minutes you'll be shouting "Let's gooooo! Out the dooooor!"

TJ's Mac and Cheese Bites

Vegetarian

Prep Time None (It's all pre-made, just take it out of the packaging)
Cook Time 20 minutes (Cook ahead of time and store in fridge)

1 (10-oz) box frozen Mac and Cheese Bites, cooked and cooled
¼ cup Three Cheese Pomodoro Pasta Sauce

Served here with: Red and green bell pepper strips (sliced thin), Ranch dressing, and Freeze Dried Strawberries.

Kelly's Tip!

Save time by pre-washing and slicing a couple days worth of celery, peppers, cucumbers, and other vegetables in advance. Store them in your fridge. Then you only have to do the packing, not the cutting, when you're trying to get out the door.

Did You Know?

The first macaroni and cheese recipe appeared in the 1824 cookbook *The Virginia Housewife* written by Mary Randolph, Thomas Jefferson's cousin. However, Randolph's recipe took much longer than five minutes to make. Pasta was made by hand in those days, a very labor-intensive process.

Five-Minute Asian Adventure

When in California, do as Californians do – enjoy a California Roll. Or, enjoy them in any state that has a Trader Joe's, because TJ's has great sushi. We love going out to a restaurant for sushi, but very few offer sushi made with brown rice. Even though our girls insist they prefer white rice, TJ's has a California Roll made with brown rice that's so good, they never mind eating the healthier version.

You can even make your own sushi in about five minutes. At our State Fair a couple of years ago, Loren bought a sushi maker in order to do just that. The demo guy with the sharp knife showed us how, and made it look like a lot of fun. Loren had a lot of fun with it at home. Twice. This is much easier.

TJ's Brown Rice California Roll

Prep Time None
Cook Time None (It's all pre-made, just take it out of the packaging)

1 pkg refrigerated Brown Rice California Roll

Served here with: Shelled Edamame sprinkled with a dash of Sesame Soy Ginger Vinaigrette and Oriental Rice Crackers.

Did You Know?

The California Roll got its name because of the avocado, which was first added to sushi in Los Angeles.

Gluten Free

Substitute soy sauce packet with tamari or gluten-free soy sauce

Five-Minute Meatloaf

Loren: "Driving around practically every day to auditions puts over 15,000 miles a year on my car. That makes it hard to get a car lease, and hard to stop for lunch. So I 'brown bag' it (although I stopped actually using a paper bag a few years ago.) A lot of people have favorite brown-bag memories. For some, it's peanut butter; for others, it's baloney. I can close my eyes and conjure up the look and taste of my mother's cold meatloaf sandwiches. My mother still makes meatloaf for me but now she uses ground turkey. TJ's has a fully-cooked turkey meatloaf with a taste of Italy because it's basted with a light marinara sauce. It's good hot or cold. When I eat it cold, it takes me back to my childhood lunches on the schoolyard: playing kickball, talking about Star Trek, and accidentally breaking my glass thermos (for the umpteenth time.)

TJ's Turkey Meatloaf

Prep Time None
Cook Time None (It's all pre-made, just take it out of the packaging)

2-3 slices refrigerated Italian Style Turkey Meatloaf (fully prepared)
1 serving Garlic and Cheese Bread Sticks (sliced into bite size pieces or in half)

Served here with: Baby carrots and a side of marinara. Marinated Artichoke Hearts would also be a great side.

The expression "Okey dokey artichokey" is popular, but should be used sparingly (if at all).

Did You Know?

Meatloaf was originally served in ancient Rome. No word on whether the mama who invented it wore a frilly apron over her toga.

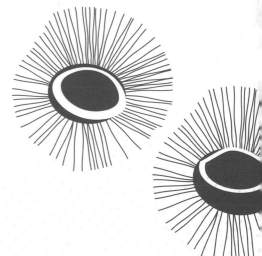

Pack it Early!

Wake up and eat

Mornings go smoother if all I have to do is wake up, pour my timer-set, pre-brewed coffee, and get myself ready for the day. I'm definitely not a fan of preparing food in those early morning hours when really, I'd rather just stay in bed. Still, we all know that breakfast is the most important meal of the day.

To cut down on morning madness, my family packs lunch at night. So why not go a step further and also prep for breakfast in the evening? Hey! You can even set the coffee timer an extra 15 minutes later if you know that lunch and breakfast are already made!

Save even more time by taking the most important meal of the day with you – on the road to school or work. (Don't forget to put a travel mug next to the coffee maker.)

Let your children know they can help themselves to a breakfast already waiting for them in the fridge. Then hit the snooze button - you still have time!

"I went to a restaurant that serves 'breakfast at any time'. So I ordered French Toast during the Renaissance." – comedian Steven Wright

Kim Gerber

As a Los Angeles mom, wife, and Children's Nutrition Advocate, I am grateful to have a voice as a proponent for the Real Food Movement. Several years ago, I noticed a decided difference in mood and behavior immediately following my children's consumption of processed food laden with artificial ingredients. I began researching and experimenting with recipes to duplicate these foods using healthy, fresh ingredients. Thus was born OutoftheBoxFood.com, a website dedicated to providing fresh alternative recipes to processed "kid food." Today, through Out of the Box Food and my participation as an ambassador for Jamie Oliver's Food Foundation, I continue to strive to help make naturally healthy food accessible and achievable for families.

Romance in a Bento

We may not all be able to lay a blanket beneath a shady tree amidst the scent of rosemary and lavender, but we can certainly enjoy the fragrant tastes of a leisurely European picnic. This breakfast bento box assembles in minutes, but allows us a slow, luxurious meal reminiscent of the flavors we'd enjoy during a European summer.

European Picnic Breakfast

Vegetarian

Prep Time 10 minutes
Cook Time 20 minutes (for hard boiled eggs)
Serves 6

6 eggs
2 loaves European artisan bread such as whole wheat or Kalamata Olive
1 artisan bread, French baguette
1 (6.5-oz) block Vintage Reserve Cheddar Cheese, divided
6 fresh Clementine oranges
3 Tbsp Fig Butter
3 Tbsp unsalted butter
1 ½ cups raw almonds
30 dried apricots (optional)
Sea salt to taste
Black pepper to taste

1   Place eggs in medium saucepan and fill with water to cover eggs by 1 inch. Bring water to low boil, and then turn off heat. Let sit for 17 minutes. Drain and refill with ice water. Once cooled, peel eggs.

2   Slice European artisan bread into 18 slices. Slice baguette into 18 slices.

3   Slice cheese into twelve ⅓-inch slices.

4   Place 3 slices European artisan bread, 3 slices French baguette, 1 peeled hard boiled egg, 2 slices cheddar cheese, and 1 Clementine in the main compartment. Sprinkle egg with sea salt and pepper. Add Fig Butter and ½ Tbsp butter sprinkled with sea salt to small compartment. Add ¼ cup raw almonds and 5 apricots to other small compartment.

Nutrition Snapshot
Per serving: 398 calories, 24g fat, 5g saturated fat, 9g protein, 41g carbs, 8g fiber, 29g sugar, 22mg sodium

Kelly's Tip!

This meal would also be delightful at an evening concert. I'd love to take this tasty assortment to the Hollywood Bowl and enjoy it with a bottle of wine, some Mozart, and good friends.

All Shook Up!

Music history buffs may already know that Elvis Presley was reported to have loved a fried peanut butter and banana sandwich. There was just something about warm bread, peanut butter, and banana that got him "all shook up." These Rock & Roll Stuffed Croissants take that rock & roll favorite and add a little Trader Joe's quality and convenience to give this classic a 21st century twist.

Rock & Roll Stuffed Croissants

Prep Time 7-9 hours (overnight to proof croissants, i.e., let them rise)
Cook Time 20 minutes
Serves 4

Vegetarian

Special Equipment: Baking sheet, parchment paper

1 (12-oz) box frozen Mini Croissants (8 mini croissants)
1 egg
8 tsp creamy salted peanut butter
2 fresh bananas, sliced into ¼-inch slices

1 Place frozen mini croissants on a parchment-lined baking sheet and leave at room temperature to rise (7-9 hours). Bake croissants according to package directions.

2 Using a paring knife, cut a horizontal slit into middle of each croissant from the side (do not cut down from the top). Fill each with 3 banana slices and 1 tsp peanut butter.

Nutrition Snapshot
Per croissant: 434 calories, 25g fat, 11g saturated fat, 11g protein, 48g carbs, 2g fiber, 12g sugar, 368mg sodium

Served here with: Fresh apple slices sprinkled with cinnamon and fresh strawberries.

Did You Know?

The whole process of making croissant dough from scratch, layering it with butter, folding and rolling repeatedly, and shaping can take the better part of two days. Certainly less fussy, and a whole lot faster would be to use frozen croissants from TJ's.

Breakfast in Paris

Who says you can't have greens at breakfast? These pre-made individual quiches are made healthier accompanied by a lightly-dressed arugula salad. Add a piping hot cappuccino, and you'll be instantly transported to a sidewalk café in the heart of Paris (if you close your eyes and let your taste buds lead your imagination).

Parisian Café Quiche

Vegetarian

Prep Time 4 minutes
Cook Time 24 minutes
Serves 4

4 individual frozen quiches (Broccoli Cheddar or Spinach & Mushroom)
2 cups arugula
½ tsp extra virgin olive oil
½ tsp freshly squeezed lemon juice
Dash sea salt
Sliced almonds (optional)

1 Preheat oven to 400° F. Place quiche on baking sheet and bake for 24 minutes. Meanwhile, toss arugula with lemon juice and olive oil. Sprinkle with sea salt and set aside.

2 Once cooled, place quiche quiche in main compartment and top with arugula salad. Garnish with sliced almonds.

Nutrition Snapshot
Per serving: 468 calories, 31g fat, 15g saturated fat, 17g protein, 32g carbs, 2g fiber, 4g sugar, 913mg sodium

Served here with: Fresh raspberries with mint, and plain Greek yogurt drizzled with honey.

Lox of Love

These Smoked Salmon Breakfast Sandwiches kick the average bagel, cream cheese, and lox to the curb. A tangy Goat Cheese & Caper Spread combined with fresh vegetables and smoky cured salmon make for a gourmet meal on the go.

Smoked Salmon Breakfast Sandwich

Gluten Free

Use Udi's
gluten-free bagels

Prep Time 12 minutes
Cook Time 3-4 minutes
Serves 4

4 bagels, halved
8 oz Wild Nova Smoked Sockeye Salmon
4 thin slices red onion
1 large tomato, thinly sliced
Goat Cheese Caper Spread (recipe below)
Spinach Topping (recipe below)

Goat Cheese Caper Spread
1 (4.5-oz) container Goat's Milk Creamy Cheese
2 heaping tsp finely chopped red onion
1 Tbsp capers, rinsed and chopped

Spinach Topping
2 cups bagged spinach, washed
½ tsp extra virgin olive oil
½ Tbsp freshly squeezed lemon juice
Dash sea salt

1 Prepare Goat Cheese Caper Spread by mixing Goat's Milk Creamy Cheese, onion, and capers. Set aside.

2 In a small bowl, prepare Spinach Topping by tossing spinach leaves with olive oil and lemon juice. Sprinkle with sea salt and set aside.

3 Lightly toast bagel halves and spread 2-3 teaspoons Goat Cheese Caper Spread onto bottom halves. Top each bagel sandwich with two slices Wild Nova Smoked Sockeye Salmon, 1 onion slice, 1 tomato slice, and ½ cup Spinach Topping. Place tops on bagels and serve.

Nutrition Snapshot
Per sandwich: 442 calories, 8g fat, 3g saturated fat, 27g protein, 64g carbs, 2g fiber, 2g sugar, 1,247mg sodium

Served here with: Fresh organic strawberries and sliced banana.

Did You Know?

Lox and smoked salmon are not the same thing. Lox is salmon that has been cured in salt, sugar and spices. Gravlax is a variation of this process, cured in salt, sugar, and dill. Scottish salmon, on the other hand, is both cured and smoked.

Pack it Early!

Brenda Bennett

I'm Italian, and I love food. Italian women know how to cook coming out of the womb. They lovingly delegate kitchen duties with a pinch on the cheek, and they eat with that same passion and gusto. Maybe they eat a bit too much, but I will get to that in a minute. I grew up watching and learning to cook from the best: my fabulous grandma, Nonna, and my mother. My happiest memories involve kneeling on a chair at a flour-covered butcher-block table, helping my grandma roll gnocchis, assemble raviolis, make banana bread, and mold pizelles.

As I grew into a young woman, my girth grew, too. The cooking and baking passion continued, but overeating and yo-yo dieting became my norm. I struggled for years, and after having two children, I decided enough was enough. I would use my lifelong love of cooking to create healthier versions of my favorite foods, without using white refined flours and sugar. This was no simple task, but I've always liked a good challenge. Maintaining the weight loss I've achieved through healthy eating, without sacrificing taste, has been my new and improved passion for the last nine years. My desire to encourage and teach others how to cook healthier, fabulous, naturally-sweetened meals is how my blog, Sugar-Free Mom (sugarfreemom.com), came to be.

I live in Rhode Island with my hunky hubby of 15 years and my three pretty picky children, ages 6, 9, and 12. There is controversy in our house as to how all three children could be so darn picky. My bet is on the hubby, but being a perfectionist myself, I know it's probably a bit of both of us. My kids are my biggest blessings in life, but the toughest food critics I have ever met. No recipe is blog-worthy unless it has been accepted and approved by them. That often means making healthy recipes a few times before they get the thumbs-up. I don't mind; it pushes me all the more. Although the cooking ingredients have changed in order to lead a healthier lifestyle, my love for family, and passion for great food, will never change.

Cake for Breakfast

Do you have picky family members? Do you often make a meal and find that one child is not as thrilled as the others because of one little ingredient you might have put into the recipe?

Well, that's my family! I like to make baked oatmeal in a 9 x 13-inch baking dish and add fruit. If I add blueberries, I have one child who will not eat it. If I make it with my favorite, raisins, none of my kids will eat it. Then there's the hubby who wants nuts, but the boys are allergic. So you see, this recipe came out of a deep desire to please everyone in my family. I want everyone to eat what I'm putting in front of them for breakfast, and I don't want to have to make three different breakfasts (which I hate to admit I've certainly done).

I knew I found a winner with this dish when my oldest, a picky 12-year-old child who hates anything that even remotely resembles oatmeal, said, "What? That was oatmeal? Wow, I really liked it! Can I have another?" The youngest little man, who is very sensitive to food texture, said, after eating one topped with chocolate chips, "Mama, that was the best oatmeal you ever made. It was like having cake for breakfast!"

The hubby and daughter were content with theirs topped with nuts, and I was smiling from ear to ear eating mine with raisins. Miracles really do still happen!

Personalized Baked Oatmeal to Go

Prep Time 15 minutes
Cook Time 30 Minutes
Serves 12

2 ½ cups old-fashioned rolled oats
1 ripe banana, mashed
½ cup applesauce, unsweetened
1 egg, beaten
¼ cup honey
1 ½ cups milk
1 tsp pure vanilla extract
1 tsp baking powder
1 tsp ground cinnamon
2 Tbsp flaxseed meal
1 tsp salt
Cooking spray
Our Favorite Toppings: semi-sweet chocolate chips, Dried Berry Medley, roasted sunflower seeds, Simply the Best Trek Mix (optional)

Use oats labeled gluten-free

1 Preheat oven to 350° F. Meanwhile, in a small bowl, combine banana, applesauce, egg, honey, milk, and vanilla extract. Set aside.

2 In a large bowl, mix together baking powder, cinnamon, flaxseed, salt, and rolled oats.

3 Pour wet ingredients into dry ingredients and mix until combined.

4 Line a 12-cup muffin pan with cupcake liners. Spray inside of each cupcake liner with cooking spray. Pour batter into muffin cups and top with desired toppings. Batter will be runny, but don't worry!

5 Bake for 25-30 minutes or until a toothpick in center comes out clean. Let rest for 5 minutes before removing from pan. Cool on wire rack. Enjoy hot or cold!

Nutrition Snapshot

Per muffin: 127 calories, 2g fat, 1g saturated fat, 5g protein, 23g carbs, 2g fiber, 8g sugar, 247mg sodium

Note: Once cooled, baked oatmeal can be stored in the refrigerator in an airtight container or frozen. If frozen, thaw overnight in the refrigerator for morning breakfast.

Served here with: Berry-topped plain Greek Yogurt with honey, and fresh mixed berries.

Did You Know? The man dressed like a Quaker on the iconic Quaker Oats box is named Larry.

Averie Sunshine

I love Trader Joe's and have been singing its praises for over three years on my blog, AverieCooks.com. Some of my favorite TJ products are their coffee, Mango Ginger Chutney, Speculoos Cookie Butter spread, and tempeh. The store is also a wonderful resource for baking supplies at a great price. I love to bake and use their 72% chocolate bars for all my melted chocolate needs. I always have a stash of semi-sweet chocolate chips for impromptu times that I may need chocolate, which, in my kitchen, happens frequently. Their bourbon vanilla extract is heavenly, and I make sure to grab a big supply of their seasonal white chocolate chips so that I have a stash to last me for most of the year. After I'm done stocking up on dry goods for baking, I top off my basket with their butter and half-and-half. Then I head home to create something gooey and sweet.

I'm a believer in the "everything in moderation" approach to eating. Although I love a big green salad with fresh, raw, crunchy vegetables, and I like to top my salads with tofu, edamame, or tempeh, I also like to save room for dessert because life is more fun with dessert included. Here I'm sharing some of my family's favorite recipes. So after you've had your spinach in the frittata, enjoy some chocolate and peanut butter, in bite-size form.

I live in San Diego, California with my husband and 5-year-old daughter. You'll usually find me in my kitchen, up to my elbows in peanut butter, butter, sugar, and chocolate, as I develop and create recipes for my own cookbook, scheduled to be released in spring 2013. When I'm not cooking, I'm probably running or doing yoga, blogging, taking pictures and working on my photography, goofing off with my family, or shopping at Trader Joe's. Say "hi" if you bump into me there; it's my second home.

Holy Frittata!

This complete vegetarian meal comes together in minutes. The variations are endless. Use whatever cheese you have on hand and vegetables taking up space in your refrigerator, then select sauces or spices you see on your shelf. Feel free to get creative. The sky is the limit on this easy protein and veggie-packed meal.

Spinach and Red Pepper Frittata

Prep Time 5 minutes
Cook Time 25-30 minutes
Serves 2

Vegetarian
Gluten Free

4 eggs
²/₃ cup frozen spinach, thawed and excess water squeezed out
¼ cup finely diced red bell pepper
Salt and pepper, to taste
2 Tbsp Hot & Sweet Pepper Jelly, available seasonally (or use Ginger Mango Chutney, Sweet Chili Sauce, or sweet & sour sauce)
Pinch chili powder
Pinch cayenne pepper
Pinch garlic powder
Pinch onion powder
¼ cup chopped carrots, green peppers, mushrooms, asparagus, green beans, onions, corn, or any vegetable you have on hand
¼ cup shredded cheese (any kind)

1 Preheat oven to 375° F.

2 Spray a medium baking dish or pie dish with cooking spray. Crack eggs into baking dish and lightly beat with a fork. Add remaining ingredients except for cheese, and stir into eggs until evenly distributed. Place baking dish on top of a cookie sheet and bake for 25 to 30 minutes, covered.

3 Remove lid, top with cheese and bake for additional 5 minutes, uncovered, to brown the top very slightly. Frittata is done when a knife inserted in center comes out clean and edges are just beginning to brown and pull away slightly from the sides of the dish. Remove frittata and slice on a cutting board, or slice directly in baking dish. Store leftovers in refrigerator and serve either cold or reheated, for up to two days.

Nutrition Snapshot
Per serving: 331 calories, 18g fat, 10g saturated fat, 21g protein, 19g carbs, 2g fiber, 16g sugar, 533mg sodium

Did You Know?

A frittata is essentially an open-faced omelet. It might be turned over during cooking like a pancake, but it is never folded in half, like its cousin, the omelet. A frittata is usually divided into slices among diners, not served whole to a single person.

Caramelized Bananas

There is something so decadent and delicious about bananas that have been cooked with a little butter, sugar, and cream. Probably because anything that is cooked with a little butter, sugar, and cream goes from ho-hum to oh-yeah-gimme-some. The best part is that these take less than five minutes, and you can use them to top pancakes, waffles, oatmeal, cereal, or just eat as is with a spoon. You won't want to miss a drop of the delicious caramelized sauce.

Prep Time 5 minutes
Cook Time 4 minutes
Serves 2

Vegetarian
Gluten Free

1 banana, sliced into rounds about ¼-inch thick
2 Tbsp brown sugar
1 Tbsp butter or margarine
½ tsp cinnamon
¼ cup heavy cream (or half-and-half, milk, nut milk)
½ tsp vanilla extract

1   Spray a non-stick skillet with cooking spray, add bananas, and cook for about 1 minute over medium-high heat, allowing them to sear.

2   Add remaining ingredients except for vanilla, and cook over medium heat, stirring gently and continuously, for about 3 minutes, or until sauce begins to thicken, reduce, brown, and caramelize. Turn off heat, add vanilla, and stir (the alcohol in the vanilla will cause sauce to bubble up, so use caution when adding).

Note: To make vegan, use margarine and a vegan milk such as almond or cashew milk. Coconut milk (full-fat recommended) will impart much more flavor but can also be used.

Nutrition Snapshot
Per serving: 182 calories, 10g fat, 6g saturated fat, 2g protein, 24g carbs, 2g fiber, 16g sugar, 18mg sodium

Served here with: Yogurt

Did You Know?

Bananas Foster is a dessert of caramelized bananas set on fire – usually tableside, if you're dining out – with a flaming shot of rum. It was created in 1951 at Brennan's Restaurant in New Orleans. Owen Brennan named the dish after his pal, Dick Foster, an integral member of the Vice Committee that cleaned up the French Quarter during that time.

Faux French Toast

If you're curious how to make French toast sticks that aren't made with any toast, make these cinnamon, sugar, and graham cracker crumb encrusted sweet potatoes. They taste like French toast but are made with potatoes. These are like a dessert in stick form because the dry rub on the potatoes turns into a lovely streusel coating.

Sweet Potato Graham Cracker "French Toast" Sticks

Prep Time 10 minutes
Cook Time 45 minutes
Serves 2 generous portions, or more based on size of sweet potato used

Vegetarian

1 large sweet potato or yam
1 egg, beaten
½ cup graham cracker crumbs
⅓ cup cornstarch
¼ cup brown sugar
¼ cup white sugar
1 tsp cinnamon

1. Preheat oven to 375° F and line a baking sheet with a Silpat liner, foil, or parchment paper (lining your sheet will save you immense headache in the cleanup process). Meanwhile, peel sweet potato, rinse with water, and slice into sticks no more than ½ inch wide (the length does not matter as much as the width).

2. In a large bowl, beat an egg with a fork and place sweet potato sticks into egg mixture and toss to coat.

3. In another large bowl, combine all dry ingredients and stir to create a dry rub. Grab a handful of egg-coated sweet potatoes and coat with dry rub, then place on prepared pan. Repeat with all remaining potatoes. If you have extra egg mixture or extra dry rub, sprinkle over top of sweet potatoes before baking.

4. Bake potatoes for 30 minutes, then flip. They will likely have become stuck to the pan, so use a spatula to separate and flip over. Bake for additional 10-15 minutes until golden and crispy. Remove from oven and if potatoes are stuck together, either tear them apart with your hands after they've cooled a bit, or place on cutting board and slice.

5. Serve with maple syrup for dipping if desired.

Nutrition Snapshot
Per serving: 562 calories, 7g fat, 1g saturated fat, 7g protein, 117g carbs, 6g fiber, 55g sugar, 522mg sodium

Note: To make vegan, replace egg with chia, "flax egg" or other liquid egg replacer.

Served here with: Clementine pieces and a container of maple syrup for dipping.

Did You Know?

The graham cracker was named after Dr. Sylvester Graham, a minister during the early 1800s. Graham was a man ahead of his time: He disapproved of bleaching flour and believed firmly in eating whole grains. He added bran and wheat germ to whole-grain flour to invent "graham flour" and, ultimately, the "graham cracker," which he believed improved health.

Fave Combo Crave

I've never met anyone who doesn't want to eat chocolate or peanut butter for breakfast or as an anytime snack. These snack balls are fast and easy to make, taking mere minutes in the microwave. If you're concerned about portion control with chocolate and peanut butter in your midst, don't worry, because this is a small-batch recipe. These are great for breakfast or as an afternoon pick-me-up. Toss a couple of these little bites into your purse or gym bag - chocolate and peanut butter is a combination you'll love anytime.

Speedy Chocolate PB & Oat Snacker Whackers

Vegetarian
Gluten Free

Use oats labeled
gluten-free

Prep Time 5 minutes (plus 10 minutes to set)
Cook Time 5 minutes
Makes 6 balls

2 Tbsp chocolate chips
2 to 3 Tbsp peanut butter (or other nut butter)
2 Tbsp milk (or nut milk)
½ cup old-fashioned rolled oats
1 tsp vanilla extract (optional)
1 Tbsp sweetener (brown/white sugar, agave, maple syrup or stevia to taste – optional)
1 Tbsp other dry ingredients (coconut flakes, chia seeds, sunflower seeds, nuts, more chocolate chips, raisins, scoop of protein powder – optional)

1 Melt chocolate chips, peanut butter, and milk together in the microwave in 30 second intervals, stirring and checking.

2 Add oats and any optional ingredients, stirring to combine. (You want this mixture to be fairly dry. If it's not dry enough to hold a shape, add more oats, one tablespoon at a time.)

3 Divide mixture into 6 pieces and roll into balls.

4 Refrigerate or freeze for 10 minutes, until mixture has set.

Nutrition Snapshot
Per ball: 83 calories, 5g fat, 1g saturated fat, 3g protein, 9g carbs, 1g fiber, 3g sugar, 28mg sodium

Note: To make vegan, use nut milk instead of regular milk.

Served here with: Papaya Spears and blueberries, granola

 **Kelly's Tip!**

Store a jar of all-natural peanut butter upside down when you bring it home from the store. When you're ready to open it, a lot of the oil will have mixed with the peanut butter, saving you labor and pesky oil spills as you stir to combine. Once opened, store the jar upside down in your refrigerator, and you won't have to stir every time you open it.

Pack it Kid Friendly!

Fun food for little fingers

In a perfect world, kid-friendly would mean more than tater-tots, mac and cheese, PB&J, and pizza. Some children are adventurous eaters; others not so much. Most children will eventually eat everything their bodies need over the course of a week. So offer up a wide variety of natural goodness, and if your child turns up her nose at something, keep trying. It may take 7-15 times of tasting a particular food before they'll actually like it.

In addition to the kid-approved meals in this chapter, there are lots of other recipes throughout the book that will likely appeal to your little eater. Be adventurous! Take them on a journey through all the pictures and see what catches their eye. If they can picture it, they may just get excited about eating it.

"It's bizarre that the produce manager is more important to my children's health than the pediatrician." - Meryl Streep

Brianne DeRosa

I like to think of myself
as a young, cool, urban-fringe
locavore. The reality is, I'm just a
working mom, neither quite as young nor as cool as I used to pretend to be,
who's trying to figure out how to get everybody fed. And by "fed," I mean preparing
a meal with as much grace, humor, taste, style, and locally, responsibly produced food as I
can reasonably achieve. Maybe it'll be healthy, too. And…oh yeah, not too pricey. Also, it must
satisfy the tastes and food moods of my loyal husband, J., and our sons, 5-year-old L. and 3-year-old
P. In other words, I spend a lot of time seeking the Holy Grail of family feeding.

I was blessed to grow up in a family where cooking was valued. By the time I moved out on my own, I had a
little notebook filled with favorite family recipes I'd recorded. I figured it would be easy to feed a family if I just
had those recipes. The truth is, modern life makes it harder to get a real-food dinner on the table at a reasonable
hour than it was back when my grandmother and even my mom were doing this. The only way I get three scratch-
made meals into me, J., and the kids every day is by planning. Lots of planning. Plus a healthy dose of improv.
That old theatre degree has got to be good for something.

"My mommy really loves me because she always packs my healthy lunch." - L., age 5, when asked by his
teachers about love.

*Brianne DeRosa hangs out at farmers' markets, talks to growers, reads reads reads about food and
agriculture, feeding kids, and eating well. She turns her family into guinea pigs whenever she gets a
chance. A classical soprano with an MFA in Theatre Education/Outreach and Dramatic writing,
she started her blog, Red, Round, or Green (redroundorgreen.wordpress.com), because
having a family gave her a point of view as a cook. Being a mother to two boys, one
with sensory-motor problems, made her even more eager to learn about
food systems and how the stuff we eat affects little people's
bodies and brains.*

Hometown Pub Grub

When I was a small child, my family lived in Buffalo, New York. I'm a proud upstate girl. (Go Bills!) Though we moved from the area before I was old enough to have made many regional food memories, I still have a soft, mushy spot in my heart for really good chicken wings and Beef on Weck. Beef on Weck is Buffalo's take on a French Dip sandwich. The beef is served on "weck," a special pretzel roll, and there's usually some sort of horseradish spread involved. Now that my 3-year-old, P., has discovered his inner carnivore and asks for roast beef morning, noon, and night, I wanted to make a grab-and-go lunch for him that would bring a taste of my roots to our New England home.

Spicy Beef Pinwheels

Gluten Free

Prep Time 5 minutes
Makes 48 pinwheels

24 slices deli roast beef (approximately 1 lb)
8 Tbsp Horseradish Hummus (or more, to taste)

1 Separate roast beef slices and lay them out with the short sides facing you. Spread 1 tsp Horseradish Hummus onto each slice of roast beef. (You may add more, to taste.)

2 Starting at the top, roll beef slices up tightly into logs. Slice each log in half to make two pinwheels.

Nutrition Snapshot

Per pinwheel: 19 calories, 1g fat, 0g saturated fat, 3g protein, 1g carbs, 0g fiber, 0g sugar, 47mg sodium

Serve in Large compartment with a side of Pumpernickel Pretzel Sticks or Everything Pretzel Slims.

Pickle Salad

Vegetarian
Gluten Free

Prep Time 10 minutes
Serves 2 (1 cup per serving)

1 English cucumber, sliced into ⅛-inch half-moons
2 medium carrots, sliced into ⅛-inch rounds
1 cup green beans, trimmed and cut into 1-inch pieces
2 Tbsp apple cider vinegar
¼ cup olive oil
1 clove garlic, roughly chopped, or 1 cube frozen Crushed Garlic
1 Tbsp honey
1 tsp salt
¼ tsp freshly ground black pepper
½ Tbsp chopped fresh dill
2 tsp poppy seeds

1 In a large bowl, combine cucumber, carrots, and green beans.

2 In a blender or food processor, combine cider vinegar, and next six ingredients (olive oil through dill). Blend on high speed for 2 minutes, until completely smooth. Pour dressing over vegetable mixture. Sprinkle with poppy seeds and toss until evenly coated. This salad gets better the longer it sits.

Nutrition Snapshot

Per serving: 354 calories, 28g fat, 4g saturated fat, 2g protein, 24g carbs, 4g fiber, 14g sugar, 1,045mg sodium

Served here with: Grapes

Did You Know?

"Buffalo Wings" get their name from the fact that they were invented in Buffalo, New York. They are not, as some might assume, taken from flying buffaloes.

Sushi A-Go-Go

My 5-year-old son, L., and I try to snag the occasional "date night" to connect with each other away from the hustle and bustle of the whole family. When we were planning a recent outing, L. asked me if I'd take him out to dinner at our favorite sushi bar. (This from a kid who doesn't eat macaroni and cheese. Ai yi yi.) We had an amazing time trying new things and talking about the very serious business that goes on in the life of a preschooler. The next day, L. told his teachers that sushi with Mommy made him feel "so special." I invented this lunch so L. could bring the feeling of our sushi date to school but leave behind the safety issues of storing raw fish and the mess and hassle of rolling my own maki!

Sorta Sushi Snackers

Prep Time Under 10 minutes
Serves 4

2 (6-oz) cans chunk light tuna
1 cup diced English cucumber
8 Tbsp Island Soyaki
1 (0.4-oz) pkg Roasted Seaweed Snack (24 pieces)

1 In a medium bowl, mix tuna, cucumber, and Island Soyaki until evenly combined.

2 If eating immediately, assemble snackers by spreading 2 tablespoons tuna mixture onto a Roasted Seaweed Snack, topping with another piece of seaweed, and repeating to make a double-decker "sandwich." If your sushi snackers will be hanging around in the lunch box, pack seaweed separately from tuna mixture to avoid sogginess.

Nutrition Snapshot
Per serving: 176 calories, 4g fat, 0g saturated fat, 23g protein, 11g carbs, 1g fiber, 8g sugar, 680mg sodium

Coconut Rice Salad

Vegetarian
Gluten Free

Substitute regular soy sauce with tamari or gluten-free soy sauce

Prep Time 15 minutes
Cook Time 15 minutes
Serves 4

3 cups cooked and cooled brown rice, preferably brown basmati
1 cup Shredded Carrots (available pre-shredded)
1 cup frozen edamame pods, cooked according to package directions and shelled
1 clove garlic, roughly chopped, or 1 cube frozen Crushed Garlic
½ cup light or regular coconut milk
Juice of one lime
2 tsp grated fresh ginger
¼ tsp salt
2 tsp soy sauce

1 In a large bowl, combine brown rice, carrots, and edamame.

2 In a blender or food processor, combine garlic, coconut milk, lime juice, ginger, salt, and soy sauce. Blend on high speed for 1-2 minutes, until smooth and creamy.

3 Pour dressing over rice mixture and toss to coat.

Nutrition Snapshot
Per serving: 256 calories, 4g fat, 1g saturated fat, 10g protein, 45g carbs, 5g fiber, 2g sugar, 457mg sodium

Served here with: Freeze-dried mandarin oranges

Did You Know?

Basmati rice is known for its fragrance when cooked. It is a longer grain and is less sticky than most other kinds of rice. Aromatic food is a proven appetite suppressant. Studies show that fragrant food is usually eaten more slowly and in smaller bites.

Southwestern Savvy

My husband, J., and I love spicy food. We're both nuts about Mexican and Southwestern flavors in particular, so every month when I create our family's meal plan, I make sure to include at least one evening of tacos, quesadillas, or fajitas. When J. finds out it's taco night in our house, he's delighted; unfortunately, to our dismay, our two boys are usually less than thrilled. Since I'm determined to get them on board, I keep trying to come up with different ways to introduce them to the flavors we love in Southwestern food. I knew I was making headway with them when they refused to try these stuffed peppers, and then gobbled them up the second I turned my back. I pretended not to notice.

Chicken Pepper Poppers

Prep Time 10 minutes
Cook Time 15 minutes
Serves 6 (4 mini peppers per serving)

24 sweet mini bell peppers
4 links Jalapeno Chicken Sausage (or any flavor chicken sausage you prefer)
1 cup shredded cheddar cheese

1 Preheat oven to 375° F.

2 Cook chicken sausage according to package directions and cool slightly. Finely dice sausage and mix with cheddar cheese; set aside.

3 Cut tops off peppers. Using a paring knife, carefully remove seeds and ribs from insides of peppers to make them hollow.

4 Stuff each pepper with about 1 Tbsp chicken sausage filling, pressing firmly into peppers. Place stuffed peppers on a baking sheet and bake for 10 minutes, just until peppers are slightly softened and cheese is melted.

Nutrition Snapshot
Per serving: 130 calories, 7g fat, 3g saturated fat, 13g protein, 5g carbs, 1g fiber, 2g sugar, 400mg sodium

Confetti Corn

Vegetarian
Gluten Free

Prep Time 5 minutes
Cook Time 10 minutes
Serves 4

2 Tbsp olive oil
1 red bell pepper, diced
½ medium onion, diced
1 (1-lb) bag frozen corn
½ tsp salt
¼ tsp black pepper
1 tsp honey
1 Tbsp fresh lemon or lime juice
2 Tbsp fresh basil, thinly sliced

1 Heat olive oil in a skillet over medium heat. Add diced onion and peppers and cook for 2-3 minutes, until slightly softened and translucent.

2 Add corn and cook, stirring occasionally, until heated through, about 6 minutes. Season with salt and pepper.

3 In a small bowl, whisk together honey and lemon or lime juice. Pour over corn mixture and toss to combine. Remove from heat. Add basil and stir thoroughly.

Nutrition Snapshot
Per serving: 180 calories, 8g fat, 1g saturated fat, 4g protein, 27g carbs, 4g fiber, 5g sugar, 309mg sodium

Served here with: Mango and berries.

Mangia Muffins

Spaghetti-and-meatballs is one of those quintessentially kid-friendly meals that always seems to evoke memories of the family table, big gatherings, and cozy togetherness. That's even if, like me, you grew up in a household where your closest connection to Italian heritage was an uncle who married in on your dad's side, and the only meatballs that ever appeared on your dinner plate were Swedish. My two boys love meatballs of all ethnicities. (See, I'm teaching them to appreciate diversity!) My 3-year-old will go to town on pretty much anything smothered in marinara sauce, including his own hand. After many wistful imaginings that a comforting spaghetti-and-meatball dinner could be made easily portable and neat, I invented these muffins. Now my guys can take their pasta on the go, even for breakfast (though I wouldn't recommend it).

Spaghetti and Meatball Muffins

Prep Time 10 minutes
Cook Time 25 minutes
Makes 18 muffins

4 cups cold cooked spaghetti or linguine, preferably whole-wheat
3 cups frozen Party Mini-Meatballs (roughly half of a 20-oz pkg), thawed and halved
2 cups marinara sauce
1 cup grated mozzarella cheese
½ cup thinly sliced fresh basil
1 cup ricotta cheese
6 eggs
1 tsp salt
Cooking spray

1 Preheat oven to 375° F. Lightly grease muffin pans (enough to make 18 muffins).

2 Roughly chop cooked pasta into small pieces, about ½ inch to one inch long.

3 In a large bowl, combine pasta pieces, mini-meatball halves, marinara, mozzarella, and basil. In a separate bowl, whisk together ricotta cheese, eggs, and salt until thoroughly combined. Pour ricotta mixture over pasta mixture and carefully fold it all together, mixing until pasta and meatballs are evenly coated.

4 Fill prepared muffin pans with spaghetti mixture (about ⅓ cup each). Bake for 25 minutes, until "muffins" are set and the tops are beginning to brown.

5 Allow "muffins" to cool slightly. Run a butter knife around edges of each "muffin" to help loosen them from pan before removing.

Nutrition Snapshot
Per muffin: 127 calories, 5g fat, 2g saturated fat, 7g protein, 13g carbs, 1g fiber, 1g sugar, 353mg sodium

Marinated Mozzarella Salad

Prep Time 5 minutes
Serves 4

8 oz fresh mozzarella balls (ciliegine or bocconcini)
1 cup grape tomatoes
3 Tbsp sliced pitted olives, any variety you prefer
1 Tbsp basil pesto, such as refrigerated Genova Pesto
1 ½ Tbsp fresh lemon juice
1 Tbsp olive oil
¼ tsp black pepper

Served here with: A side of marinara sauce and berries.

Did You Know?

It's hard to find spaghetti with meatballs in Italy. It's primarily an American invention created here by Italian immigrants.

1 In a medium bowl, combine mozzarella balls, tomatoes, and olives.

2 In a small bowl, whisk together pesto, lemon juice, olive oil, and black pepper. Pour over mozzarella mixture and toss to coat.

Nutrition Snapshot
Per serving: 188 calories, 15g fat, 6g saturated fat, 13g protein, 4g carbs, 1g fiber, 0g sugar, 207mg sodium

Kelly's Tip! EasyLunchboxes are great for homeschoolers, too. Pack lunches the night before. At lunchtime, the kids can help themselves and their teacher can take a much-needed break!

Pack it Kid Friendly!

"There is no single effort more radical in its potential for saving the world than a transformation of the way we raise our children." – Marianne Williamson

Katie Brandow

I'm a mom who enjoys balancing work and family; playing with our kids and squeezing in date nights. I always make our health a priority. Yoga, cooking, and running are my standby sanity savers! Simply put, in all areas of life, you get out of it what you put into it. I learned this lesson early on, and it surely applies to parenting.

Prior to becoming a parent, I didn't realize how passionate I would become about my kids' nutritional needs and the impact nutrition can have on the earth. When we pack lunch, we take into account exposure to a variety of foods, clean eating, a nut allergy, a family of girls, and a dad who eats the stereotypical manly portions of food.

Just like many families, we get busy. To consistently meet our goals, we have to shop for the right foods and prepare them for easy eating at home and on the go. At the same time, we want minimal mess, little waste, and no allergens. Advanced planning allows us to meet these goals with ease in no time. We make it part of a fun, family routine. The outcomes are amazing. You get what you put in, and fortunately, we can make nutrition and nutritional impacts a priority, without a huge investment of time, thanks to the EasyLunchbox System and Trader Joe's.

Daughter Neve (7 years old): "My lunch is the healthiest lunch in my class. Healthy means there isn't sugar in it, right? Can you get me yogurts with jokes, though? I'm always jealous of kids with tubes of yogurt with jokes on them. Or just leave me a love note, because I miss you when I'm at school." My reply: "I think Trader Joe's sells yogurt tubes. I hope they have jokes on them."

Katie Brandow is the President of School of Enrichment, Inc., (schoolofenrichment.com), an early childhood program in Bend, Oregon, supporting children and parents in becoming the best they can be.

Kabobs and Popcorn, of Course!

My husband and I fell in love with food on a stick during a pre-parenthood Thailand adventure, and so the tradition continues. I don't think there is anything my kids enjoy eating more than food skewered on a stick, and I'm not talking about corn dogs. When paired with popcorn, these kabobs make a healthy, easy to prepare, travel-proof snack. Traveling near and far is always more enjoyable when we have food at hand.

Savory Kabobs

Prep Time 10 minutes
Serves 2

4 (1-oz) pieces Nitrate Free Turkey Slices, rolled up
4 oz low-fat smoked Gouda cheese, cubed
1 small granny smith apple, cubed
8 grape tomatoes

1 Alternate ingredients on four small skewers.

Nutrition Snapshot

Per serving: 229 calories, 10g fat, 7g saturated fat, 24g protein, 11g carbs, 2g fiber, 6g sugar, 1,414mg sodium

Popcorn with Kale Sprinkles

Prep Time 10 minutes
Cook Time 10-12 minutes
Serves 2

1 ½ cups popcorn, such as Organic Popcorn with Olive Oil
¼ bag pre-cut kale pieces
1 Tbsp olive oil
1 Tbsp soy sauce
1 Tbsp shaved Parmesan, Romano, and Asiago Cheese blend

Substitute regular soy sauce with tamari or gluten-free soy sauce

1 Preheat oven to 375° F. Meanwhile, wash and dry kale, cutting off thicker stems. Place in single layer on baking sheet.

2 Whisk together olive oil and soy sauce. Brush mixture over kale pieces and bake for 10-12 minutes or until crisp. Remove from oven and let cool for 10 minutes.

3 Place half of the kale chips in a large sealable container and crush chips with your fingers. Store the other half in a closed container for up to 7 days of weekday snacking.

4 Add popcorn and cheese to crushed kale. Put lid on and shake (get the kids to help!). Serve into silicone liners and place in the small compartment.

Nutrition Snapshot

Per serving: 141 calories, 10g fat, 2g saturated fat, 3g protein, 9g carbs, 2g fiber, 0g sugar, 366mg sodium

Arch. of
the Recherche

Served here with: Cubed artisan French bread baguette

Kelly's Tip!

If you air-pop your own popcorn, spray the un-popped corn with olive oil and sprinkle with salt before popping. The exploding kernels will spread the oil and salt evenly.

Did You Know?

You don't have to waste the un-popped popcorn if you use a microwave oven. My daughter Julia won first place at her 4th grade science fair by proving it's possible to pop almost every single kernel. Popcorn pops when the moisture inside each kernel becomes overheated. Some kernels have less internal moisture than others. These holdouts might require two or three trips to the microwave, but almost every single kernel will eventually pop. Here's how: To prevent burning, always turn off the microwave when you hear the popping stop. Remove the popped kernels and put the "old maids" back in the microwave using a microwave popcorn maker. (Never re-use the original bag.) Keep going until you've made enough popcorn, or until you become bored with the process.

Sushi & Salad

My kids love to say they eat sushi, even if it is made with peanut butter. We incorporate peanut butter into my youngest daughter's diet almost daily, per our doctor's recommendation. She is severely allergic to tree nuts and has a slight allergy to peanuts. Because the peanut allergen levels are so low, her doctor suggested she eat peanuts daily so she doesn't become more allergic to them. (Do not follow this advice without your doctor's recommendation.) Although we were nervous about this routine at first, the doctor was right: She's never had a reaction to peanuts. Let's just say it's a good thing she likes peanut butter! Still, we have to get tricky to keep things fresh and new. Be sure to include a reusable fork.

PB&J "Sushi"

 Vegetarian

Prep Time 5 minutes
Serves 2

1 sheet Lavash Bread
6 Tbsp all natural peanut butter
4 Tbsp Organic Superfruit Spread

1   Lay lavash bread out and spread peanut butter evenly. Layer Superfruit Spread on top of peanut butter.

2   Roll lengthwise and slice sushi style. This works best when flatbread is at room temperature.

Nutrition Snapshot
Per serving: 485 calories, 26g fat, 5g saturated fat, 15g protein, 47g carbs, 7g fiber, 19g sugar, 168mg sodium

Salami & Smoked Cheeses   Gluten Free

Prep Time 3 minutes
Serves 1

2 slices nitrate free salami
2 (½-oz) slices low-fat smoked mozzarella
2 (½-oz) slices low-fat smoked Gouda

1   Layer each ingredient, starting with salami, two times, for a total of 6 layers.

Nutrition Snapshot
Per serving: 260 calories, 19g fat, 10g saturated fat, 22g protein, 1g carbs, 0g fiber, 0g sugar, 1,110mg sodium

Served here with: Prewashed, bagged organic spinach leaves with raspberries and low fat balsamic vinaigrette.

Did You Know?

• Lavash is a flatbread that is baked in a clay oven. It is most likely Armenian in origin.

• Peanut butter is so nutritious that it's the main ingredient of Plumpy'nut, an edible paste used to fight malnutrition throughout the world.

Banana Love Note with Pancakes

I confess that I write a love note to my first grader almost every day. Boy, was she surprised when her most recent note arrived in the form of a banana. It's so easy to do! Just write your note on a banana with a toothpick. As the fruit browns, the note appears. She thinks it's magic!

Of course, children need more than love and a banana to get through the day. I tuck the love-note banana in the large compartment of her EasyLunchbox container and place a small snack of roasted seaweed in the remaining space. (Give seaweed a chance. The first few times we had it we were not fans, but after a few tries, it became a staple for lunch at home and away.) Then I add some tummy-filling pancakes.

My kids eat pancakes for breakfast, lunch and dinner. Our latest favorite recipe is oatmeal, coconut, and blueberry pancakes. We freeze and refrigerate these in the EasyLunchbox containers for ready-made meals.

To keep lunchtime for eating rather than for preparing food, I cut up the pancakes, thawing them first if they are frozen. I include dipping sauces in separate containers.

Some of our favorites are Trader Joe's Organic Applesauce, Trader Joe's 100% Organic Maple Syrup Grade A, and Trader Joe's Valencia Peanut Butter with Roasted Flaxseeds.

Oatmeal Blueberry Pancakes

Prep Time 15 minutes
Cook Time 5 minutes
Serves 8

1 ½ cups whole wheat flour
½ cup all-purpose flour
4 Tbsp brown sugar
4 Tbsp baking powder
1 tsp salt
1 tsp cinnamon
3 cups quick cooking oats (or grind old-fashioned rolled oats in food processor)
4 cups unsweetened light or regular coconut milk
6 eggs, beaten
½ cup unsweetened applesauce
1 cup fresh or frozen blueberries (reserve to fold in last)

1   Preheat griddle at medium to high heat. Mix first 6 ingredients (2 types of flour, sugar, baking powder, cinnamon, salt) in bowl.

2   Mix next 4 ingredients (oats, coconut milk, eggs, applesauce) in separate bowl.

3   Combine wet ingredients with dry ingredients, mixing slowly. Once thoroughly combined, fold in blueberries.

4   Butter griddle and add batter, using a ladle. Flip when batter starts to bubble.

Nutrition Snapshot
Per serving: 354 calories, 8g fat, 4g saturated fat, 12g protein, 60g carbs, 7g fiber, 13g sugar, 423mg sodium

Note: These freeze well or can be refrigerated for up to 5 days.

Served here with: Dipping sauces.

 **Kelly's Tip!**

If you don't have a banana, or if you have writer's block, you can do an online search for "printable lunch box notes". You'll find lots of free ones with fun sayings and cute graphics. Just download, cut out, and tuck your surprise in your kid's lunch box.

Pack it
Kid Friendly!

Lori Jewett

I am a full-time life insurance agent, a full-time housewife, a full-time mom, a part-time blogger at pinknpunchy.blogspot.com, a room mom, an elementary school yearbook administrator, and I serve on the PTA. I also pick up hobbies like they have magnets attached....wheeeeeww! That doesn't leave much time to accommodate my 5-year-old daughter's high maintenance diet. She has a severe intolerance to all artificial food dyes.

I learned some cooking from my Mamaw in Arkansas, and now, with my husband by my side, I am continuing to improve my skills. He and I have a great time cooking together, and we love to combine fun ingredients to make our own recipes. Bento seemed like a good way to get our daughter to try new foods because if it's fun-looking, it better-tasting, right? That's when I found EasyLunchboxes. Soon after, a friend introduced me to Trader Joe's and its amazing selection. Now we have a quick and easy source for dye-free, all-natural foods to design fun bentos for our daughter.

Octo Family

Taia loves under-the-sea lunches and generally everything ocean-themed! Of course, it all started with Ariel, the Little Mermaid. This lunch features natural blue-dyed whole-grain rice, octo-dogs, plums, carrots, fish made from Trader Joe's Organic Fruit Wraps, and Trader Joe's Multigrain Pita Bite Crackers. I saw the octo-dogs online a few years ago and have been making them for a happy kiddo ever since. We like to use Trader Joe's All Natural Uncured All Beef Hot Dogs.

Deep-Sea Dogs

Gluten Free

Prep Time 5 minutes
Cook TIme 20 minutes
Serves 4

1 cup whole grain rice
¼ tsp all natural powdered food dye* (or more if desired)
2 hot dogs

1 Boil rice according to the box recipe. About halfway through, add ¼ tsp food dye and mix thoroughly. Keep in mind that "natural blue" is more of a purple.

2 Place rice into large compartment of EasyLunchbox.

3 Boil 2 cups of water. Meanwhile, cut hot dogs as follows: cut one in half and one into quarters (6 pieces total). Slice each piece lengthwise into 8 "tentacles," leaving the last ½ inch of each portion uncut. When water reaches a boil, drop hot dogs in for about 45-60 seconds. Scoop them out when legs start to curl. There you have your octo-dogs!

Nutrition Snapshot

Per serving: 266 calories, 9g fat, 4g saturated fat, 7g protein, 36g carbs, 2g fiber, 1g sugar, 233mg sodium

Served here with: Carrots, plums, fish cut from an organic fruit wrap, and Multi-grain Pita Bite Crackers

*Note: My favorite natural food dye is made by Chocolate Craft (chocolatecraftkits.com). Another good brand is India Tree Natural Colors, available on Amazon.com.

 Kelly's Tip!

The right combination of protein and carbohydrates can improve your child's brain function. But if that combo includes a fruity bowl of sugar and Red dye #40, um, not so much! Many children and adults are extremely sensitive to artificial food dyes. Consider switching to dye-free powders, gels, and foods. You can find a great selection online at chocolatecraftkits.com and naturalcandystore.com. And of course, anything with the Trader Joe's logo is free from ALL artificial ingredients - colors, flavors, and preservatives!

Under the Seashells and Starfish

When I first saw the Trader Joe's Organic Shells and White Cheddar Macaroni and Cheese, I thought of an under-the-sea lunch. Then I started putting one together. It ended up as more of a fun, whimsical sea creature lunch, minus the ocean! But it was delicious. I added my new favorite ingredient, Trader Joe's Kefir, in place of milk to make it even healthier. (I'm hooked on the stuff because I love the flavor it gives my meals.)

Mac and Cheese with Dogs and Peas

Prep Time 5 min
Cook Time 12 min
Serves 4

1 (6-oz) box Organic Shells and White Cheddar Macaroni and Cheese
5 Tbsp (1% milkfat) Lowfat Plain Kefir
3 turkey hot dogs, cooked per package directions
½ cup frozen peas

1   Boil 6 cups water. Stir in pasta and return to a boil. Cook 8-10 minutes. Drain. Add kefir and organic cheese packet. Mix until cheese is evenly distributed.

2   Slice hot dogs into ⅛-inch slices. Hand-cut with a knife or use a mini star-shaped cutter to cut each slice into a starfish. If meal will be served warm, microwave for 20 seconds.

3   Microwave frozen peas for 30 seconds or until warmed.

4   Place shells in EasyLunchbox. (The amount will vary from child to adult meals.) Top shells with starfish and peas.

Nutrition Snapshot
Per serving: 203 calories, 8g fat, 3g saturated fat, 15g protein, 33g carbs, 2g fiber, 0g sugar, 794mg sodium

Served here with: Freeze Dried Fruits, Gourmet Jelly Beans (natural and dye free), and mandarin orange segments.

Pack it Kid Friendly!

Rachel Beard

As a parent of two young children, I have made it my mission to model healthy eating and exercise habits for my family. A key part of my strategy is packing healthy lunches for them to eat at school every day. As a busy working mother, I was initially very intimidated by the task. I lacked ideas and vision for their lunch boxes, so I turned to Google to find inspiration. I quickly became enamored with bento bloggers. It turns out there are lots of moms out there who pack lunches every day with simple, fresh ingredients. But they add a little flair to make the food more enticing. I drew up some ideas, ran to the store, and was making my own fun and healthy lunches in no time.

This adventure has become a huge success. My kids love their special lunches. I am thrilled to send them off with a special meal every day. Even their teachers and classmates enjoy checking out the lunches. Now I do my own bento blogging on Rachel's Random Ramblings (rachelsrandom.com). Best of all, this idea is contagious. Several parents have told me they packed a bento lunch and got their kids to eat more fruits and veggies as a result. I love the idea that I am helping others while helping my own family live a healthy lifestyle.

"I love the special lunches my Mommy makes for me because they come from my home, they are healthy, they are pretty and fun, and they taste like my Mommy loves me! And we do love each other very much!"
- Lily, age 6

Oh Tommy, I Love you so!

I'll bet you think this is a re-imagining of the Famous California Tommy's Original Burger, right? Wrong! It's actually inspired by the Texas Tommy, a "special night at the diner" favorite of mine I relished as a kid. Texas Tommies are hot dogs stuffed with cheese, all wrapped up with greasy, gooey, drippy bacon. Yum! Here's my vegetarian take on that old and unhealthy version. My California-born kids love it.

California Tommy Dogs

Prep Time 10 Minutes
Cook Time 14 minutes
Serves 8

1 (8-oz) pkg refrigerated Crescent Rolls
1 (12-oz) pkg Lightlife Smart Dogs
4 slices Morning Star Bacon Strips, cut in halves
2 slices cheddar cheese, cut into rectangular quarter strips
Ketchup or mustard for dipping

1 Preheat oven to 375° F. Meanwhile, unroll crescent dough in 4 rectangular sections. Press each rectangular section together to join them and also flatten dough. Make a cut down the middle of each section to make two smaller rectangles, 8 total.

2 On each rectangle, place a bacon-strip half, a cheese-strip quarter, and a Smart Dog. Stretch dough around hot dog, ensuring the ends meet. Press edges together to form a seal.

3 Bake for 14 minutes, or until golden brown. Serve whole, or cut into bite-size chunks.

Nutrition Snapshot

Per serving: 178 calories, 8g fat, 4g saturated fat, 13g protein, 14g carbs, 1g fiber, 4g sugar, 628mg sodium

Served here with: Strawberries, Big & Chunky Apple Sauce, Kettle Corn Cookies, carrots, edamame hummus, and mustard.

Did You Know?

The Texas Tommy (grilled hot dog with bacon and cheese) was actually invented in Philadelphia. The Coney Island Dog (chili dog with mustard and onions) was actually invented in Detroit. The Chicago Dog (poppy seed bun with pickles, peppers, tomatoes, neon green relish, mustard, and celery salt) on the other hand, was actually invented in Chicago.

THANKS for GIVING me this lunch!

I originally designed this meal for the kids, but found that my husband liked it even more than they did. This delicious and simple meal is reminiscent of Thanksgiving leftovers, but can be made at any time of the year.

Turkey-Day Pinwheels

Prep Time 10 Minutes
Cook Time None
Serves 2

2 whole wheat tortillas
¼ cup Neufchâtel cheese (or low-fat cream cheese)
1 Tbsp dried cranberries
4 slices turkey deli meat

1 Spread 2 Tbsp Neufchâtel cheese on each tortilla.

2 Top with ½ Tbsp organic dried cranberries, sprinkling all over cream cheese to distribute evenly. Add 2 slices turkey to each tortilla. Roll up tortillas into a log-shaped wraps. Seal edge with a little cheese if necessary.

3 Slice logs and arrange pinwheels in the lunch boxes.

Nutrition Snapshot

Per serving: 262 calories, 10g fat, 4g saturated fat, 20g protein, 27g carbs, 4g fiber, 4g sugar, 318mg sodium

Place turkey pinwheels in container next to cheese triangles in a silicone muffin cup. Include Monkey Business Trail Mix in additional silicone muffin cups in large compartment.

Served here with: Strawberries, snow peas, and hard-boiled egg.

Did You Know?

Another name for pinwheel is "whirligig," which is a truly fun word to try and work into a conversation.

I ♥ Pizza Lunch

This fun recipe can be used for dinner one night and lunch the next day. My kids like it because they get to customize their own meals and make a huge mess at the same time. Anything involving rolling pins is generally a hit at my house. Feel free to swap out the Canadian bacon and pineapple for whatever toppings your family prefers.

Heart-Shaped Pizza

Prep Time 10 Minutes +20 Minutes for dough to warm on counter
Cook Time 12-16 minutes
Serves 6

1 (1-lb) bag refrigerated Whole Wheat Pizza Dough
¾ cup refrigerated pizza sauce
1 ½ cups part-skim shredded mozzarella cheese
4 slices Canadian bacon
½ cup pineapple chunks

1 Unwrap dough and leave at room temperature for 20 minutes.

2 Preheat oven to 425° F. Meanwhile, divide dough into 6 pieces. Roll out each piece and use your hands to stretch out tops to form heart shapes. Use plenty of flour to ensure dough does not stick.

3 Add 2 Tbsp pizza sauce to each dough heart and spread well to cover dough. Sprinkle ¼ cup cheese on each pizza.

4 Use a small cookie cutter to make fun shapes (stars, hearts, whatever your kids like) out of the Canadian bacon and put those on top of cheese. Add chunks of pineapple. Bake in oven for 12-16 minutes, or until cheese is bubbly and dough edges golden brown.

Nutrition Snapshot
Per serving: 245 calories, 5g fat, 1g saturated fat, 12g protein, 37g carbs, 4g fiber, 3g sugar, 1,029mg sodium

Served here with: Grapes, blueberries, strawberries, orange bell peppers, and a hard-boiled egg.

Kelly's Tip!

To get stinky smells out of a lunch bag, dampen a paper towel, piece of bread, or a rag in white vinegar, and put it in the bag overnight.

Pack it Playful!

Eye-appealing meals to bring out the kid in all of us

Something about compartments makes food irresistible to kids. The makers of those colorfully packaged Lunchables figured that out a long time ago. Here we've created meals that add fun and whimsy to good nutrition. You can make your own eye-appealing "Momables" with a little bit of imagination and creative effort. Lunchtime is more fun when it's playful!

"A smiling face is half the meal."
- Latvian Proverb

Bobbi Jo Fleischman

Two years ago I weighed over 270 pounds. Fed up with being overweight, I changed my life by switching to healthy foods and exercise. After getting myself under the 200-pound mark, I turned my attention to my three young daughters. I wanted to instill healthy eating habits in them, also. I stumbled across EasyLunchboxes in my search for healthy lunch ideas. It was as if the heavens opened up! They are my go-to lunch containers. I have enjoyed making healthy meals with them ever since.

My oldest daughter loves school lunches. I, on the other hand, completely dislike them. I do not think children should be served processed patties and nuggets every day. That's why I started making her lunches cute and appealing — I was competing with pizza and mini doughnuts. An EasyLunchbox container, a couple of cookie cutters, and some yummies from Trader Joe's go a long way when it comes to rivaling processed food. When I'm trying to decide what to pack in my daughters' lunches, my motto is, "When in doubt, put a face on it."

Visit my blog, Bobbi's Bentos (bobbisbentos.blogspot.com) to see more of my fun meal ideas.

Dog Gone It!

Although I have a ginormous collection of cookie cutters, I really dislike making cut-out cookies. Almost none of my cookie cutters has ever touched cookie dough, aside from a couple of random Christmas cutters. Instead, I use them for sandwiches. My cookie cutter collection has grown tremendously since I began making bento lunches. It takes so little effort to punch a sandwich into a shape, and the effect is big. I have found that some breads work better than others, and the same goes for the fillings. Here are a couple of tips I've learned along the way: Try flattening your bread first if it's one of the varieties that doesn't cut well. Depending on your filling choice you might have to cut each layer independently and then assemble.

Dog and Bone Sandwiches

Vegetarian

Gluten Free

Use gluten-free bread

Prep Time 10 minutes
Serves 1

2 slices bread
1 Tbsp Cocoa Almond Butter
Chocolate Covered Sunflower Seed Drops
½ oz cheddar cheese

Tools:
Dog sandwich/cookie cutter
Bone sandwich/cookie cutter
Small heart cookie cutter
Small letter cookie cutters

1 Cut two dog and two bone shapes out of bread slices. Spread Cocoa Almond Butter on one of each shape.

2 Before placing the top slice on top of its match, punch out the word dog on the bone using letter cutters and a heart using a heart cutter on the dog. Assemble both sandwiches.

3 The dog's ear and nose are Chocolate Covered Sunflower Seed Drops.

4 Using a knife, cut cheese in shapes to make sunshine. Place items in large compartment.

Nutrition Snapshot
Per serving: 305 calories, 12g fat, 3g saturated fat, 10g protein, 35g carbs, 8g fiber, 14g sugar, 300mg sodium

Served here with: Chopped yellow plums and Chocolate Covered Sunflower Seed Drops. Blue Jell-O.

TweetHeart

I love making cute food for my daughters to eat. I also have an obsession with putting faces on food. The more ways I can think of sneaking healthy food into them, the better. Cucumber eyeballs are way cooler to eat than cucumber slices. A sandwich with a side of veggies is a good lunch. But turn those same items into a sweet bird, and now it's an irresistible lunch to a kid. When I go to my kitchen to pack lunches for the next day, I usually have no idea what the end product will be. I start by opening my fridge and checking to see what's hiding in there. Then I figure out how to put a face on it.

Birdie Sandwich

Use gluten-free bread

Prep Time 15 minutes
Serves 1

2 slices bread
1 slice cheese
3 baby carrots
2 cucumber slices
Chocolate Covered Sunflower Seed Drops
Any sandwich filling you prefer (PB&J, meat, cheese)

Tools:
Oval sandwich/cookie cutter
Small circle sandwich/cookie cutter

1 Make your child's favorite kind of sandwich using 2 slices of bread. Cut sandwich into an oval shape using a cookie cutter or knife. Place sandwich in large compartment.

2 To make wings and a beak, cut shapes out of sliced cheese with a knife. Two triangle shapes make a great beak.

3 Use a small circle cutter or a knife to make eyes out of cucumber slices. Add two tiny carrot pupils. I like making cross-eyed faces.

4 To make bird feet, use a knife to slice baby carrots in various lengths.

5 To make bird feathers, slice a flat piece of baby carrot lengthwise with a knife and then cut little notches in it.

6 Assemble pieces on the oval sandwich to make a bird. Add sunflower seeds to the bottom of the compartment.

Served here with: Apple slices. Two varieties of different colors make an eye catching alternating pattern. Alternate peeled and unpeeled cucumber slices to make stripes.

Kelly's Tip! Kids love things mini-sized. Save those little taster spoons they give you at the yogurt shop, or purchase a few inexpensive baby spoons to include in their lunch box for things like yogurt. They'll eat it up!

Pack it Playful!

Cristi Messersmith

I grew up in British Columbia, Canada, but I moved to the United States 17 years ago, when I married my husband, an American sailor and my best friend. We spent several years in New Orleans, where the first of our five little ones was born. We then moved Whidbey Island, Washington, where we've been lucky to be stationed for the past 10 years. We love the Pacific Northwest.

I was a very picky eater as a child, and I still am. Admittedly, I have not exposed my kids to a wide variety of foods, so it's no surprise that they are picky, too. When they started school, I packed their lunches with readily available, pre-packaged, kid-friendly foods. We slipped into a junk-food-lunch rut.

I soon realized I wanted something better for them, and thought maybe their packed school lunches could be an opportunity for healthier eating. They'd be hungry, their options would be limited to what I'd packed, and I'd be too far away to hear them complain!

Of course, I didn't really want to give them anything to complain about. Instead, I wanted to pack them nutritious, well rounded, appealing meals they would enjoy eating. I searched the Internet for ways to make wholesome food fun, and that's how I discovered bento and many of the blogs whose authors are also featured in this cookbook. They inspired me with the countless creative ways they packed and presented nutritious meals. Eager to try my hand, I resolved to stop sacrificing my kids' nutrition for convenience. I started my own bento lunch blog, Bent On Better Lunches (bentonbetterlunches.com), to help me stick to that resolution.

Many of the bento blogs I enjoyed featured meals packed in EasyLunchboxes. I thought my kids would love them, so I ordered some and got started. I was surprised by how easy it was, and how much fun, both for me as a way to express creativity, and for my children, who began to look forward to their fun lunches. In turn, they did start trying new things. Healthy foods they previously shunned were suddenly fun to eat, now that they were cut in cute shapes or displayed as part of a theme. I also think that taking the time to make lunch just a little bit special lets them know their meals were made with love. I hope the lunches in this cookbook inspire you the way I was inspired.

Stop For Lunch

Like most children I know, my little ones like cars, trucks, and roads. When driving with me, they love shouting out the color of the traffic light, and whether I should stop or go, so I knew they'd like this lunch theme. My 5-year-old said it was a good thing I made the traffic light in the right order so she didn't have to stop until she ate the tomato!

If your kidlet doesn't care for mustard or mayo, a dab of honey or peanut butter also works to stick the wheels to the bread. And if you use red apples, or if your apples tend to brown too much for your kid's liking, you could peel just the road lines instead of the other way around.

Transportation Sandwich

Vegetarian
Use vegetarian
deli slices

Gluten Free
Use gluten-free
bread

Prep Time 5-10 minutes
Serves 1

2 slices bread
2 slices ham (or other deli meat)
2 large slices cheese
Condiment like mustard, mayo, or even butter – to affix wheels
Quarter apple
Green grapes
Grape tomatoes
Thick slice of cheddar cheese – about ¾-inch thick and big enough to cut two 1-inch circles

Tools: Paring knife. Small circle cookie cutter (about 1-inch), vehicle shaped cookie cutters, long food picks, drink stir sticks or wooden skewers, cut to fit if necessary.

1 Cut vehicles from bread using cookie cutter, 1 of each vehicle per slice. Cut vehicles from cheese slices. Fold ham to size of vehicle. Assemble sandwiches. Cut wheels from excess cheese, or use another slice. Attach to bread with condiment.

2 With paring knife, lightly score shape of road lines just through the peel, across the apple quarter. Beginning where you have scored, carefully peel rest of apple leaving only the road lines. Spray with lemon juice to keep from browning.

Nutrition Snapshot
Per serving: 465 calories, 14g fat, 7g saturated fat, 34g protein, 52g carbs, 7g fiber, 3g sugar, 1,020mg sodium

Served here with: Grapes, tomatoes, and cheese on picks.

Dino Love

These dinosaurs are too happy to go on a rampage. They're in love, and will soon be a mama and daddy dinosaur. See their fruit-leather hearts and the grape baby dinosaur eggs in the nest? See that pile of mozzarella cheese bones that are toys for the babies? These parents-to-be are nesting!

Cutting shapes from fruit leather is an easy, yummy, and nutritious way to add some cuteness to a kid's lunch. If it's not sticky enough on its own, use a dab of honey as glue.

Dinosaur Sandwiches

Use gluten-free bread

Prep Time 5-10 minutes
Serves 1

3 or 4 slices bread, depending on size of dinosaur cookie cutters
2 Tbsp peanut butter
1 stick mozzarella string cheese
Desired amount of grapes
2 Tbsp raisins
1 leaf lettuce
Fruit leather (optional but cute)

Tools: Dinosaur cookie cutter, spoon, muffin cup (optional, for a colorful "nest")

1. Cut 4 dinosaur shapes from bread. Spread 2 with peanut butter, top with remaining 2. Line largest container with lettuce leaf. Arrange dinosaurs atop lettuce "jungle." Sprinkle raisin "dirt" beneath them. Cut 1 raisin in half, pinch, and poke each piece into dinosaur sandwiches as eyes.

2. Slice mozzarella string cheese in half lengthwise. Using a spoon, slice the lengths diagonally to make curved "rib bones." Place in smallest compartment.

3. Line small compartment with a muffin cup, or more lettuce, to make the dino "nest". Fill with grape "dinosaur eggs." For a cute touch, cut tiny hearts from fruit leather and affix to dinosaur sandwiches with honey or peanut butter "glue."

Nutrition Snapshot
Per serving: 490 calories, 22g fat, 6g saturated fat, 25g protein, 49g carbs, 20g fiber, 24g sugar, 538mg sodium

Kelly's Tip!

Include a little note in your child's lunch box to say, "Good luck on the test today!" or "I love you!" Or maybe include a silly cartoon you found in the newspaper. Your child will know you're thinking of them, and may even surprise YOU with a note somewhere unexpected!

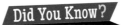

Did You Know?

The fact that reptile meat (such as rattlesnake) tastes like chicken, combined with strong evidence that modern birds are direct descendants of dinosaurs, has led scientists to conclude that dinosaurs probably tasted like chicken.

Patterns Patterns Everywhere

My preschoolers like patterns and repetition. Their favorite early-math workbook activities involve patterns and sequencing. And patterns make for an eye-catching lunch!

I made this lunch when my girls had friends over for a playdate. The patterns made the lunch assembly line easier too! Lunch was a hit with all the girls and their friends. They loved the polka-dot pizzas best.

Patterned Pizza

Vegetarian

Use vegetarian
hot dogs

Prep Time 10-15 minutes
Cook Time about 5 minutes
Serves 1

1 English muffin
2 each of several small fruits (such as grapes & tomatoes)
Spoonful pizza sauce
Desired amount of shredded mozzarella cheese
5-6 pepperoni slices or thinly sliced hot dogs
¼ each of 2 kinds of apples (such as Granny Smith & Gala)
1-inch-wide slices of 2 kinds of melons (such as cantaloupe & honeydew)
Lemon juice

Tools: Paring knife, drink swizzle sticks or wooden skewers, cut to size if needed

1   Spread pizza sauce on English muffin. Top with shredded cheese. Arrange meat slice polka dots, evenly spaced. Toast in toaster oven until cheese is melted, about 5 minutes.

2   While pizza is toasting, skewer grapes & tomatoes on drink swizzle sticks, both in the same order.

3   Slice apples into wedges, trim to fit container if needed. Spray with lemon to prevent browning. Arrange in stripes, alternating between peel colors and peel side up or down.

4   Arrange melon pieces in side compartment.

Nutrition Snapshot
Per serving: 352 calories, 12g fat, 4g saturated fat, 16g protein, 48g carbs, 8g fiber, 12g sugar, 1,027mg sodium

Hugs & Kisses

This was the first picnic lunch I packed in our EasyLunchbox containers. I was taking my sproutlets to a big playground and wanted a meal they didn't need to sit down and eat all at once. I wanted them to be able to nibble, run back and play some more, and come back for more food later - a bit like a party platter. I decided on crackers, ham and cheese, because they go well together stacked or on their own, apple wedges because I love tart apples and sharp cheddar cheese together, and baby carrots because the girls love them and we needed a vegetable.

The containers were perfect. The compartments kept the foods separate until we were ready to eat them: no soggy or broken crackers, no crumb-covered cheese. Cutting the ham and cheese into bite-size hearts, Xs, and Os seemed like a fun way to put a little gender-neutral love into the lunch that would make my girls smile, yet wasn't too cutesy for my boys.

Ham and Cheese "Hug-a-bles" Lunch

Gluten Free

Use gluten-free crackers such as Savory Thins

Prep Time 5 minutes. (It takes me about 15 minutes to cut all the pieces and pack the food for 4 lunches!)
Serves 1

Half an apple
1 serving (3 oz or 8-9 pieces) baby carrots
Desired amount of cheddar &/or white cheddar cheese
6 crackers
Desired amount of thickly sliced ham (thin would still work, but thicker is easier to cut and looks better)
Lemon juice (for dipping apples so they don't turn brown)

Tools: Paring knife. Small cookie cutters. I used a heart, x, and o

1 Cut apples into wedges. Dip in cold water or lemon juice to prevent browning. Arrange in a row. Arrange baby carrots beneath apples.

2 With cookie cutter, cut cheese hearts, x's and o's with cookie cutter, arrange atop carrots.

3 Cut ham into hearts, x's and o's, place in small compartment.

4 Add a dash of love :)

Nutrition Snapshot
Per serving: 318 calories, 11g fat, 6g saturated fat, 24g protein, 31g carbs, 5g fiber, 11g sugar, 772mg sodium

Served here with: Crackers

 **Kelly's Tip!**

If you like to include a napkin in your child's lunch box, why not make your own? Colorful 12-inch cotton fabric squares, finished with simple folded corners, can be made extra fun by hand embroidering. Or use fabric ink to stamp silly phrases, initials, or a nickname.

Pack it Playful!

JeeJee Donham

Food creation and healthy eating are very important in my life. While living in Japan and studying for my master's degree in international law, I took on a part-time job in a sushi restaurant in Niigata. I wanted to learn more about food preparation in Japanese culture. Sushi is mastered by achieving a balance of technique, thought, and placement. When most people cook, they don't think deeply about the components that are used and how to place them.

I learned that the key to creating food is fresh, healthy ingredients, placement and love. The food we eat and serve represents our inner self and becomes part of the people who consume it. I have taken this philosophy and applied it to my family and our way of living. My husband and I now own a large online bento site, BentoUSA.com. We provide the tools needed to express love for food creation, and offer inspiration to eat healthy food joyfully. I also use bento creations as a tool to engage with my family. We work together and make spectacular, healthy, fun foods to share and enjoy.

When I am not working or in the kitchen creating bento art, I can be found around town with my husband, looking for new ideas for fun creations. Living in San Francisco allows me to experience many unique cultures and foods. During my lunchtime, I love to sit by the Bay and eat a healthy lunch while watching the world around me. On weekends, my husband and I often make creative lunches together. Then we'll take them on a picnic and enjoy the wonderful San Francisco weather.

"I'm always surprised each day, by what new creations I'll find in my lunch!"
    - JeeJee's husband

Afternoon Jungle Delight

Sandwiches are the usual go-to lunch box choice for many people. They're easy to prepare, convenient, and don't require heating. But sandwiches can get tiresome and less appetizing if you always eat the same ones. So I make my family's sandwiches full of pizazz and cute surprises each day, turning the everyday meal into something fun and appetizing for the ones I love. I always create different cutout cheeses on top of my sandwiches, depending on what inspires me at the time.

Jungle Sandwich Lunch with Curried Chicken Salad

Prep Time 15 minutes
Cook Time 20 minutes (for hard-boiled egg)
Serves 1

¼ cup refrigerated Curried White Chicken Deli Salad
Small peas
1 egg
Baby romaine lettuce
1 hot dog bun with sesame seeds
1 slice ham or turkey
1 slice cheddar cheese, cut in half
1 slice jack cheese, cut in half
1 Tbsp mayonnaise
4-5 broccoli florets
Carrots, cut into ½-inch slices and then cut into eighths lengthwise
1 cherry tomato
Ranch salad dressing (or your favorite dressing)

Tools: Egg Yolk Mold Kit, Bento Cutter, Bento Food Picks, Bento Food Cups

1 Fill small compartment with chicken salad. Place peas around chicken salad to create a frame for the flowered hard-boiled egg. Make flowered shape hard-boiled egg, using egg yolk mold kit and following package directions. Slice a small flower shape. Use a bento stem pick to make the stem for the flower.

2 Line the largest compartment with lettuce. Fill bun with ham, ½ slice cheddar, and ½ slice jack. Cut in half. Using bento cutters, cut remaining cheese into a lion shape and a mini butterfly body and wings. Using two types of cheese will add color and contrast. Place two bento food picks for the antennas of the butterfly (and to help keep the sandwich together).

3 Place broccoli florets across the bottom and dressing in a bento food cup. For fun, put two bento alphabet food picks, saying "HI," into dressing or sandwich. Place carrots and small cherry tomato into a bento food cup and include a bento pick for easy dipping into dressing.

Served here with: Blueberries and strawberries.

Nutrition Snapshot
Per serving: 816 calories, 48g fat, 16g saturated fat, 41g protein, 55g carbs, 9g fiber, 19g sugar, 1,213mg sodium

Did You Know?

"Curry" comes from the word "kari," which means "sauce" in the Indian subcontinent. Now you know not to order "curry with sauce on the side." It wouldn't make sense!

Hola Sombrero Burrito Man

My husband goes crazy over Mexican food. He can eat it everyday. When we go out for Mexican food, he always orders a burrito and freshly made guacamole with chips. I make him a Mexican lunch often and I spice it with a touch of fun to make him smile. Who can resist a cheese man with a sombrero? My husband prefers his food spicy, so I make his Burrito Man with the hottest salsa I can find. For those like my husband who aren't happy until they are literally "crying from the spicy," be sure to add chopped chiles to the guacamole.

Bean and Rice Burrito and Fun Sombrero Man

Vegetarian

Prep Time 20 minutes
Serves 1

1 frozen 99% Fat Free Bean & Rice Burrito, prepared according to package directions
Veggie & Flaxseed Tortilla Chips
¼ cup Hot Chipotle Salsa
¼ cup guacamole
Sliced Cheddar cheese
Sliced Jack cheese
Sliced cucumber skin
1 small pea
1 cherry tomato
Romaine lettuce

Tools: Alphabet Cutter, Bento Cutters, Bento Food Picks

1 Line largest compartment with romaine lettuce. Place burrito on top of lettuce. Use bento cutter or knife to cut Cheddar and Jack cheeses into burrito man shape: face, body, arms, feet, mustache, and bow tie. Using two types of cheese will add color and will give a nice contrast to the food. Place a pea on the face as a nose of the burrito man. Place a bow-tie bento food pick to enhance your creation. Cut 2 pieces of cucumber skin and lay down to create the sombrero hat shape on top of the cheese cutout.

2 Fill up the space of the largest compartment with color tortilla chips to give more of a festive feel. You can use other color chips as well if you like.

3 Cut tomato in half. Insert cheese in the middle of tomato to make tomato cheese sandwich. Connect tomato and cheese using leaf food picks. Put tomato cheese sandwich in the middle of Guacamole in the small compartment.

4 Pour Hot Chipotle Salsa in the smallest compartment. Cut cheddar cheese using Alphabet bento cutter to read HOLA. Carefully place the HOLA cutout cheese on the salsa.

Nutrition Snapshot
Per serving: 694 calories, 91g fat, 11g saturated fat, 33g protein, 76g carbs, 12g fiber, 5g sugar, 641mg sodium

Did You Know?

"Chipotle" is the Spanish word for 'smoked chili pepper'. Most people think it means "burrito wrapped in foil."

Pack it Playful!

Jenn Christ

I started making cute lunches for my son when he started the first grade. I knew I did not want him to eat the cafeteria food, but I also didn't want him to feel like he was missing out on anything. Having taken some Japanese classes in college I knew a little bit about bento lunches, and they seemed to be the perfect thing. Searching for ideas, I found a community of bento bloggers, and that got me blogging my own creations. I started out pretty simply and the lunches have grown more elaborate through the years. I knew I was truly bento-obsessed when I planned a family road trip and carefully scheduled stops near stores that carry bento supplies. True story. You can read more about my bento obsession on my blog, Bento for Kidlet, at http://www.bentoforkidlet.com/

My son is almost finished with elementary school. I know that there's a good chance he won't want cutesy lunches pretty soon, but so far I am still getting away with it. Of course, now that he's older he also requests much more complicated designs, but his unfailing belief in my abilities spurs me on. I enjoy every lunch I make and feel good knowing he is getting a healthy boost in the middle of the day, as well as a serving of fun!

Super-Star Lunch

My child is a super-star, and I like to make him feel that way every time he opens his lunch. I like to use clever designs to let him know that I'm thinking about him before I send him off to school. I want him to have a healthy lunch that's filled with love.

Star-Shaped Sandwich

Vegetarian
Use vegetarian deli slices

Gluten Free
Use gluten-free bread

Prep Time 10 minutes
Serves 1

2 slices soft whole wheat bread
1 slice deli meat
2 slices cheddar cheese
2 tsp mayonnaise, divided
1 tsp mustard
3-4 strips yellow bell pepper, sliced in strips lengthwise

Tools: Large star shaped cookie cutter. Star shaped food picks. Small letter shaped cookie cutters.

1 Cut bread into a star shape with cookie cutter; repeat with second slice of bread. Cut meat and cheese with cookie cutter to fit sandwich. Spread 1 tsp mayo and mustard on either slice of bread and put meat and cheese in between.

2 Cut cheese to spell out the words "Super Star" and affix to sandwich with a dab of mayo to keep letters from moving.

3 Place finished sandwich in large compartment and place 3-4 strips of bell pepper behind the star to mimic a "shooting tail."

Nutrition Snapshot
Per serving: 453 calories, 16g fat, 7g saturated fat, 29g protein, 50g carbs, 6g fiber, 0g sugar, 946mg sodium

Served here with: Blackberries and star shaped picks, pea pods, and Yogurt Stars.

Pack it Playful!

Lise LaTorre

A few careers ago, I was a nanny. I loved adding tidbits to the kids' lunches to make them fun: a peek-a-boo window here, a scalloped edge there, and always a little note on the napkin. Fast-forward a couple decades. Now I am the proud mother of C., a vivacious, playful, active vegetarian preschooler who eats a lot more of her lunch if it's fun. I started with the touches I did ages ago for the other kids, but as I searched online for vegetarian lunch ideas for kids, I became increasingly interested in the beautiful bentos I saw there.

In addition to being C.'s mom (and wife to the endearingly sweet D.), I am a full-time web developer with a passion for making things fun and interesting for my family. Bento-ing started with just trying to get C. to eat more (and have fun at the same time), but now it's become my favorite obsession, er, hobby. I love the challenge of finding a cute illustration and turning it into food, keeping its likeness and personality intact. Some lunches are easy and some turn out to be a lot of work, but every time C.'s face lights up when she sees that day's lunch, I start getting excited about the next one.

I hold myself accountable by trying to post every lunch to my blog, Veggie-Bento.com. Knowing that I will be sharing the result of my efforts helps keep the creativity and inspiration flowing. I hope we inspire you to have fun too!

"Lise has a new creative outlet with bento that perfectly marries her flair for fun and joy with her innate sensibility for packing stuff into grids (she makes websites for a living). Every morning she sets herself new puzzles to figure out, only this time they are in cheese and bread, rather than ones and zeroes." – D.

Take Me to Your Leader

I get my inspiration from a wide variety of sources: cake decoration, manga, coloring books, cartooning, and most of all, the loads of other examples online, especially from the other bloggers featured in this book.

For this lunch, I found a cartoon of aliens and thought it would make a fun lunch. I was struck by the thought that an egg is the perfect shape for a spaceship. The lunch all came together from there.

"Remember that sparkle in the eye you get when you've just made something creative and fun that you're really proud of? Lise got that sparkle back when she started making bento lunches for our daughter." -D

Alien Lunch

Vegetarian

Gluten Free

Use gluten-free bread

Prep Time 30 minutes
Serves 1

2 slices whole grain bread
2 slices white cheddar cheese
Condiments (optional)
2-3 drops of natural food dye
Fruit leather
2 strands uncooked spaghetti
2 hard-boiled eggs
Kiwi
Pineapple

Tools: Circle, oval and star cookie cutters, 2 food picks, paring knife

1. Make sandwiches with one piece of cheese and 2 pieces of bread. Using cookie cutters, cut out 2 large ovals and 4 small circles and arrange them according to the photo. If you will be transporting your lunch, connect sandwiches with dried pieces of spaghetti. For extra cuteness, add another layer of cheese on top of the sandwiches and rub natural food dye into the cheese. To make a fun face, cut out two more small cheese circles and two smaller circles and one small semi circle of fruit leather. Add two little food picks to resemble antennae.

2. Take a peeled hard-boiled egg and cut in half length-wise. Cut one half length-wise and one width-wise so you end up with two long semi-circles and two domes. Take one dome piece and one longer piece and connect using an uncooked piece of spaghetti. Add two smaller pieces of spaghetti for the other feet of the spaceship. You can decorate your spaceship with mustard dots and/or fruit leather topper.

Nutrition Snapshot

Per serving: 466 calories, 19g fat, 8g saturated fat, 30g protein, 47g carbs, 6g fiber, 0g sugar, 730mg sodium

Served here with: Veggie Stix and kiwi, pineapple cut out into star shapes.

Did You Know?

People who study the phenomenon of crop circles and believe they're made by aliens are called "cereologists." Doesn't that sound like someone who should be studying Raisin Bran?

Aquarium in Your Lunch

I came up with this lunch on a day that C. clearly woke up on the wrong side of the bed. I figured a smiley crab just might make her a little less crabby. One of my favorite parts of this lunch is the aquarium salad. C. devours her carrots and cucumbers as she catches the fish.

"Lise's language of love is based on a vocabulary of nutritious, vegetarian food. And although there's a love note in every lunch box, the heart of the matter is in the eating." -D

Crabby Sandwich

Prep Time 30 minutes
Serves 1

2 slices whole grain bread
2 Tbsp almond butter
1 banana
1 strand uncooked spaghetti
Fruit leather

Tools: Circle cookie cutters. If unavailable, use a bottle, glass, or small jar.
Fish shaped egg mold. Paring knife.

1 Slice half the banana into thin circles and set aside. Using cookie cutters
(or alternative tools if unavailable) cut out the following from bread slices:
- 2 large circles
- 4 medium sized circles
- 4 small circles
- 2 rounded strips of bread. You can make these strips by cutting out a large circle, then moving the cutter down a bit and cutting again. Repeat one more time. These will be your crab legs.

2 Assemble bread circles into sandwiches by coating each with a thin layer of almond butter and placing banana in between. Make sure banana slices are fully covered in almond butter to prevent browning. Arrange sandwiches in the shape of a crab in the largest ELB compartment, using pieces of uncooked spaghetti to hold them together. By lunchtime, the spaghetti will soften so you don't need to worry about any sharp pokes when eaten. Decorate with fruit leather eyes and smile with a dab of jelly or almond butter to help them stick.

Nutrition Snapshot
Per sandwich: 171 calories, 6g fat, 1g saturated fat, 5g protein, 26g carbs, 4g fiber, 4g sugar, 120mg sodium

Aquarium Salad

Ranch dressing, or your favorite salad dressing
French green beans or baby spinach leaves
Sliced cucumber
Sliced carrots or orange bell pepper

1 To make an aquarium salad in the smaller compartment, lay down a thin layer of your favorite salad dressing. Carefully place several pieces of "seaweed" cut from green vegetables; French green beans work best, but spinach leaves sliced in tall thin triangles work well too. On top of the seaweed, position your favorite veggies cut out in the shape of fish. If you don't have a fish-shaped cutter, you can make the body from an oval with a notch cut out and a triangle for the tail.

Molded Hard-Boiled Egg "Fish"

1 egg, hard-boiled and peeled
1 cup hot water
2-3 drops natural food dye

Vegetarian
Gluten Free

For a fun egg-fish in the smallest compartment, heat a mug of water colored with natural food dye. Soak a peeled, hard-boiled egg in the hot water until the desired color, then pop into a fish egg mold. I usually do this step first, and then stick it into the freezer until I am done with the rest of the lunch. Then, I pop it open, slice the egg in half, and place it in the smallest compartment.

Did You Know?

In Japan, there is a popular trend called Kyaraben, which is the art of shaping food into popular cartoon characters or super heroes.

Pack A Snack!

When you need a little sumthin' sumthin'

Sometimes you don't need to pack a complete meal. When you're on the go, a little DIY snack may be just the thing to keep you or your child going. So long, vending machines!

Kendra Peterson

I started making creative lunches when my eldest daughter, Z., was almost two. I saw some fantastic ideas online to make food fun just by using cookie cutters so I figured I could give it a try. All I had at that point was a set of mini Christmas cutters, so I took the gingerbread man and cut out some cheese. In hindsight, I should have called them "cheese men" rather than letting Z. name them. But she loved her "man cheese," and that got me hooked on making her food more fun and interesting.

I started using bento boxes around the same time. I would like to tell you I did this because I was disgusted by the waste of plastic baggies and that I was looking out for the environment. The truth is, I was tired of shelling out money for something I planned to throw away. Plus, I kept running out of bags because I was too lazy to go shopping.

Not only did I start saving money, I also noticed I started packing healthier lunches. Having all those spaces to fill made me stop and think about what was missing. I found myself aiming to incorporate something from each important food group. My daughter was more open to trying something new if it was in one of her "beautiful lunches," as she started calling them. Now we're both eating healthier. Occasionally she'll even surprise me with a request for more vegetables or by choosing something new at the grocery store.

I live in the Seattle area with my hubby, and our two little princesses, Z. (now four), and E. (still a baby). I spend my time chasing the girls around, making cute foods and blogging about it at Biting the Hand That Feeds You (bitingmyhand.blogspot.com). I try not to burn down the house as I attempt to cook using actual ingredients. I spend my free time planning creative lunches, blogging about other stuff, and catching up on Facebook. And buying more bento gear.

Twisted Snacker

There is nothing I hate more than laboring over food only to create a colossal disaster. Using TJ's premade bread dough means I don't have to plan ahead to bake something creative. Instead, I can use my time to experiment with different shapes and flavors. Since my eldest daughter is an olive fiend, I figured these twists would be a popular snack. I make some in advance, keep them in the fridge, and then let them warm to room temperature in our EasyLunchbox containers for an after-school snack. A lot of our snacking is done in the car as we shuttle between activities.

Through trial and error, I have found that my EasyLunchbox containers are easiest for both of us to use on the go. For me, they stay on my lap while I sit around in the car or a lobby waiting for her class to end. For her, they're big enough to fit on her lap without sliding off a leg while riding in the car, but not so big that they don't fit between the armrests of her car seat. When I'm feeding or holding the baby, I like packed snacks that are easy to eat one-handed, and that don't get my fingers too messy, which was part of my inspiration for these fun treats.

Olive-er Twists

Vegetarian

Prep Time 5-10 minutes
Cook Time 10-12 minutes
Makes 6 twists

1 (8-oz) can refrigerated Crescent Rolls
2 ½ Tbsp canned chopped black olives (¼ of a 4.25 oz can)
Up to 2 Tbsp extra virgin olive oil, divided
1 cup finely grated cheddar cheese, divided
1 ½ tsp Italian seasoning, divided
½ tsp garlic powder
⅛ tsp salt

1 Preheat oven to 375° F. Meanwhile, in a small bowl, combine chopped olives, 2 tsp olive oil, ½ cup grated cheddar, and 1 tsp Italian seasoning. Set aside.

2 Unroll crescent roll dough. Using a pizza cutter or knife, cut dough in half width-wise (making two short fat rectangles, rather than two long skinny ones).

3 Spread olive mixture evenly over half of the dough. Cut both halves of dough into 6 strips (12 strips total), each about 1-inch wide.

4 Place each strip of plain dough over olive-covered dough and press together gently, pinching ends together if possible. Pick up each pair of strips and gently twist a few times. Place on parchment paper-lined baking tray.

5 Brush twists with remaining olive oil. Sprinkle on remaining grated cheese, remaining Italian seasoning, garlic powder, and salt. Bake for 10-12 minutes.

Nutrition Snapshot
Per twist: 189 calories, 12g fat, 6g saturated fat, 8g protein, 15g carbs, 0g fiber, 4g sugar, 743mg sodium

Served here with: Basil pesto, Crunchy Curls, kiwi flowers, and mandarin orange segments.

Kelly's Tip!

Instead of using expensive, pre-packaged snack foods, you can make your own snack boxes. Buy food in bulk: You will save money, and your little ones will enjoy helping you fill up a few EasyLunchbox containers at a time with just the right amount of snacks. These are great to keep in the pantry, ready to go for a last-minute outing or a hungry toddler at home.

Did You Know?

Most black olives that you purchase are actually green olives that have been dyed via a curing process, in order to can them. The natural colors of olives are either green or purple.

Accidental Goodness

Granola bars can be such a healthy snack. Plus, they fit nicely in a lunch box. Store-bought bars are either too expensive, full of junk, or tasteless. Homemade bars are economical and can be as healthy as you choose to make them. They can also be shaped to fit a theme, which is a huge plus for me.

I found an easy recipe, but I had to improvise when I discovered I had only white chocolate chips on hand. I veered from the recipe again when my brain stopped working and I accidentally tossed in a cup of each add-in. Happily, I bumbled upon a mouthful of chewy deliciousness! I love using my EasyLunchbox containers for these bars. The rigid plastic shell protects the food inside while keeping moist items away from crunchy ones.

Heavenly Cranberry Granola Bites

Prep Time 5-10 minutes
Cook Time 20-25 minutes
Hands-off Time 5 minutes
Serves 8

Vegetarian
Gluten Free
Use oats labeled gluten-free

3 cups quick-cooking oats
1 (14-oz) can sweetened condensed milk
2 Tbsp butter, melted
1 cup flaked coconut
1 cup sliced almonds
1 cup white chocolate chips
1 cup Orange Flavored Cranberries or other dried cranberries

1 Preheat oven to 350° F. Meanwhile, line a 9 x 13-inch pan with parchment paper, making it long enough to come up the shorter sides to be used as "handles" later. Grease any un-papered areas.

2 In a large bowl, combine oats, sweetened condensed milk, butter, coconut, almonds, chocolate chips, and cranberries. Mix with your hands until well blended. Press flat into prepared pan.

3 Bake for 20 to 25 minutes, depending on how crunchy you want them. Lightly browned just around the edges will give you moist, chewy bars.

4 Let cool for 5 minutes. Using a knife or cookie cutters, cut into bars, squares, or fun shapes. Carefully lift granola slab out using parchment paper "handles" sticking up at sides. Let cool completely before serving.

Nutrition Snapshot
Per serving: 527 calories, 21g fat, 9g saturated fat, 25g protein, 72g carbs, 5g fiber, 48g sugar, 85mg sodium

Note: If you want crunchy bars but custom shapes, take the pan out early, leave the granola slab in the pan and use your cutters, then put them back in for the rest of the time. You might need to use the cutter again after, but it will be much easier, and less likely to break up your shapes.
Use parchment or wax paper to separate the bars that are being stored for later.

Served here with: Strawberries cut into hearts, cheddar and mozzarella cheese cut into heart shapes using a mini cutter.

Did You Know? Granola was originally called "granula," and it was invented in the United States. The name was changed to "granola" by Dr. John Harvey Kellogg, who also invented corn flakes. Although granola was popularized by hippies in the 1960s, it was invented in the 1860s.

Chipper Dipper

Any way I can get my daughter to put a veggie in her mouth is another step towards growing a healthy eater. Dips are a fun way to make this happen. She says she doesn't like broccoli, but I know she will eat it as long as there is dip. Her favorites are ketchup and salad dressing, but hummus is much healthier. And because hummus isn't very runny, there's no fear of anything leaking if, say, one of her EasyLunchbox containers happens to get dumped on its side out of reach while I'm driving. (Which is apparently more likely than I would have thought, the way I drive!) Now, to get her to warm up to dipping in hummus, I had to give her something she wanted to eat.

Hummus Dip

Vegetarian
Gluten Free

Prep Time 5-10 minutes
Hands-off Time 60 minutes
Serves 8

2 (15-oz) cans chickpeas (garbanzo beans), drained and rinsed
½ cup extra virgin olive oil
1 Tbsp lemon juice (or juice from half a lemon)
3-4 cloves garlic, crushed, or 3-4 cubes frozen Crushed Garlic
¾ tsp salt
½ tsp dark sesame oil (add a little more if using light sesame oil, and slightly less olive oil)
¾ tsp ground cumin
½ tsp black pepper
¼ cup water, separated

1   Combine all ingredients except water in a food processor and process until smooth. Add half the water and process again. Chill in food processor container in refrigerator for at least one hour.

2   Remove from fridge and put back on food processor base. Mix again. Slowly add remaining water and mix in pulses until you reach desired consistency. You may not need to add all of the water.

Nutrition Snapshot
Per serving: 200 calories, 14g fat, 2g saturated fat, 5g protein, 15g carbs, 5g fiber, 1g sugar, 366mg sodium

Lavash Crisps

Vegetarian

Prep time 5-10 minutes
Cook Time 5 minutes
Serves 1

1 sheet Lavash Bread
2 Tbsp extra virgin olive oil
5 tsp grated Parmesan cheese
½ tsp Italian seasoning
Pinch salt

Kelly's Tip!

Kids love to dip! Pack salsa, hummus, yogurt, or salad dressing for dunking their sandwiches, veggies, or fruit. If the dip is runny, pack it in a separate, sealed container to avoid leaks. EasyLunchbox containers aren't leak-proof.

1. Preheat oven to 425° F. Meanwhile, in small bowl, combine Parmesan cheese, Italian seasoning, and salt. Set aside.

2. Using a knife, kitchen shears, or cookie cutters, cut lavash bread into desired shapes. Shapes wider than 1 inch work best.

3. Lay bread shapes onto parchment-paper-lined baking tray. Brush with olive oil (you may need slightly more or less than 2 Tbsp olive oil, depending how liberally you use it). Sprinkle cheese mixture evenly onto bread shapes.

4. Bake for 5 minutes. (Scraps and shapes thinner than 1 inch should be checked at around 3 minutes cooking time, since they crisp up faster.)

Nutrition Snapshot
Per serving: 489 calories, 30g fat, 5g saturated fat, 11g protein, 44g carbs, 4g fiber, 0g sugar, 603mg sodium

Note: I like to make fun shapes to go with a party or meal theme, which means I get a lot of scraps. I cook up the scraps too, and put them on a salad. Yum! You can also use this same recipe with tortillas or non-pocket pita bread, but the lavash bread is much easier to cut with cookie cutters.

Served here with: Assorted veggies (carrots, green beans, bell pepper strips, and cucumber).

Did You Know?

Tahini is an Arabic word for sesame paste, which, along with mashed chickpeas, lemon juice, salt, garlic, and olive oil, is the traditional recipe for hummus.

Don't Be a Chicken!

I started cooking classes for kids as a way to get the children in my moms' club to try new foods. I've found that kids who are involved in making their food tend to be more willing to try something new. They'll get excited about actually eating new foods, too. It was very fulfilling to see picky eaters enjoying something they wouldn't have touched otherwise.

Once, for a no-cook class in the park, I decided to make chicken salad. Because it was no-cook, I gave each child their own little bowl and a single serving of chicken and mayonnaise to mix. (That way, everyone could participate, but we wouldn't all have to share "the dish of a thousand fingers.") I also had a variety of healthy add-ins for the kids to choose. One child added a little of all of them, but then didn't want to eat it, so he gave his concoction to me. It was delicious! I gobbled it down and ended up making it again for myself with the leftover ingredients that evening. I found I preferred it on crackers, versus bread. Crackers make the meal a snack, and the smaller size is more fun for my preschooler to eat. Also, with my EasyLunchbox containers, I don't have to worry about the crackers getting crushed by something else in my bag.

Accidental Chicken Salad   Gluten Free

Prep time 5 minutes or less
Serves 4

1 (16-oz) pkg frozen Just Chicken, thawed*
3 to 5 Tbsp mayonnaise
¼ cup grated carrots
¼ cup raisins
¼ cup chopped celery
¼ cup chopped apple**
Salt to taste
Black pepper to taste

1 Chop and/or shred chicken into small pieces and put into medium-size bowl. Add mayonnaise and stir, one tablespoon at a time, until desired consistency is reached. (I prefer the mayo to just moisten the chicken. Others like it goopier.)

2 Add carrots, raisins, celery, apples, salt, and pepper. Mix well.

Enjoy in a sandwich, lettuce wraps, or on crackers. Omnomnom.

Nutrition Snapshot
Per serving: 273 calories, 12g fat, 2g saturated fat, 30g protein, 9g carbs, 1g fiber, 6g sugar, 322mg sodium

* You can use canned chicken here, which is easier as it doesn't need much shredding, if any. If using the 12.5-oz cans of chicken at Trader Joe's, reduce the amount of mayonnaise to 2 to 4 Tbsp.

**You may notice that apples begin turning brown after being sliced. Vitamin C helps prevent this, so sloshing them in any juice containing Vitamin C first (and then draining out the juice) will help them look fresher longer. I prefer apple or pear juices, rather than lemon, because they don't alter the flavor of the apples.

Served here with: Organic Trek Mix with Chocolate Chips, Almonds & Cranberries, Sesame Rice Crackers, and string cheese sliced width-wise into coins.

Pack it Yummy!

Great meals for every age, every day

"There is no sincerer love than the love of food."
– George Bernard Shaw

Marla Meridith

I grew up on Long Island, New York, and now live in Southern California. My favorite place on earth is Telluride, Colorado. The bigger the mountains, the better! Thankfully, both Cali and Colorado have big blue skies and lots of natural light for photography. I keep very active and love skiing, surfing, yoga, hiking and Pilates. As someone with a Type A personality, I'm a firm believer that the more you do, the more you get done; I don't do "lazy" days. I am a proud mom to two kids who keep me really busy, and wife to a husband who often acts like a big kid.

I love to shoot and style photographs of food, life, and everything in between. I got into recipe development and the love of photography after my kids were born. I noticed how essential it is to eat homemade meals for great energy and health. Real, whole food tastes best, and we celebrate it every day. I pack lunches for my kids because it is one of the most nurturing things I can do for them.

Shooting this book was a joy and one of the largest projects I have ever accepted. Crossing the finish line of this marathon photography assignment - photographing all the meals in this book - was liberating. It gave me the drive to do more fun projects like it. (I don't use the word "marathon" lightly: I've run three of them).

You can learn more about me, try out my recipes, and have fun with the food, lifestyle, and travel photos on my blog, FamilyFreshCooking.com. You can also visit my photography portfolio at MarlaMeridith.com.

ABC Pockets

There is something fabulous about being able to hold a meal in your hands. These mini pita pockets are the perfect size for kids and just as wonderful for adults. Beware: They may be small, but they are hard to stop eating. Make a few for lunch and a few more for a snack. Why ABC? Avocado, Bacon, and Cheese of course! Use any cheese you like, but slightly sharp cheddar is a classic pairing with the bacon and creamy avocado.

Bacon-Cheesy Whole Wheat Pita Pockets

Prep Time 5 minutes
Cook Time 10 minutes
Serves 4

8 Mini Whole Wheat Pita Pockets
4 oz grated cheddar cheese or your favorite cheese
4 slices Uncured Turkey Bacon or Fully Cooked Uncured Pork Bacon, cut in half
1 avocado
1 lemon, juiced

1 Cook bacon until crisp. If using fully cooked bacon, heat and crisp according to package directions. Blot bacon with paper towels. Meanwhile, slice avocado and toss pieces with some lemon juice to prevent browning.

2 Stuff mini pita pockets with cheese, avocado and cooked bacon. Toast stuffed pita pockets a few minutes until cheese is melted and gooey.

Nutrition Snapshot

Per mini-pita: 295 calories, 13g fat, 4g saturated fat, 21g protein, 29g carbs, 7g fiber, 0g sugar, 654mg sodium

Served here with: Snapea Crisps, fresh strawberries, and Go Raw Trek Mix.

Did You Know?

Cured bacon is bacon that has been soaked or packed in salt.

A Bit of Country Chic

People say I am a little fancy and a little bit country. I suppose that's what happens when a gal from Long Island spends a good part of the year in Telluride, Colorado. This quinoa is a blend of chic meets rustic comfort food. One of our favorite sources of protein is flavorful sausage. We especially love these slightly smoky, spicy ones. Feel free to use any of your favorite varieties. This dish is well balanced and perfect for a lunch box, but you can also pass it off as a tasty elegant meal for guests.

Quinoa with Asparagus and Sausage

Gluten Free

Prep Time 5 minutes
Cook Time 20 minutes
Serves 4

1 cup uncooked Tricolor Quinoa (any color you have will taste great!)
1 bunch fresh asparagus, trimmed and cut into 1-inch pieces
Sea salt
2 Tbsp extra virgin olive oil, divided
1 (12.8-oz) pkg Smoked Andouille Chicken Sausage, or 4 links of other sausage
1 lemon, juiced
Herbs for garnish (optional)
Lemon zest for garnish (optional)

1 Bring a large pot of water (enough to cover asparagus) to a rolling boil. Add a few pinches of sea salt.

2 Meanwhile, rinse quinoa and cook according to package directions. Fill a large bowl with water and ice.

3 Add asparagus to boiling water. Cook for about 3 minutes until asparagus is bright green and tender. Immediately drain asparagus in a strainer and halt the cooking process by dunking & swishing asparagus in ice water. Leave it in the water while you cook sausage.

4 Heat 1 Tbsp olive oil in grill pan over medium heat. Add sausages and cook until brown, turning occasionally, about 5 minutes.

5 Remove asparagus from water and pat dry with a clean towel. Toss asparagus with lemon juice and remaining olive oil. Plate asparagus and sausage over a bed of quinoa. Garnish with herbs or lemon zest.

Nutrition Snapshot

Per serving: 429 calories, 18g fat, 3g saturated fat, 30g protein, 38g carbs, 6g fiber, 4g sugar, 962mg sodium

Served here with: Plain Greek yogurt sweetened with Stevia and topped with fresh strawberries, Chocolate-covered Espresso Beans, and banana chips.

Did You Know?

Andouille is pronounced "ahn-DWEE." The Andouille sausage originated in France but was made famous in the United States via Cajun cooking. The word can also be hurled as an insult in French circles.

Gobble Gobble It Up!

Not sure how and why meatloaf became one of the ultimate comfort foods, but most folks enjoy this hearty meal. It ignites cozy feelings and gives you great go-get-'em energy. Around here, we go-go non-stop. This meatloaf is lighter than your grandma used to make, but it has all of the great flavor. You can dress it up a bit with some micro greens or simply top it with your favorite tomato sauce.

Our Favorite Turkey Meatloaf

Prep Time 10 minutes
Cook Time 50 minutes
Serves 8

2 lbs ground turkey, mix of white and dark meat
¾ cups bread crumbs
½ tsp onion powder
½ tsp garlic powder
Few pinches coarse ground black pepper
2 Tbsp chopped fresh herbs, such as thyme or oregano
1 large egg, whisked
2 Tbsp Soyaki
½ cup canned diced tomatoes
½ cup Organic Marinara Sauce

1 Preheat oven to 375° F with the rack in the middle. Meanwhile, combine turkey with bread crumbs, onion powder, garlic powder, pepper, and herbs. Make a well in the center and slowly add egg, Soyaki, and tomatoes. Mix with hands until well combined. Make a mound in the center of a casserole dish and cover loosely with aluminum foil. Bake for 40 minutes.

2 Remove foil and top meatloaf with marinara sauce. Bake uncovered for another 10 minutes until meat is cooked through.

3 Serve over quinoa, rice, or pasta.

Nutrition Snapshot
Per serving: 259 calories, 11g fat, 3g saturated fat, 23g protein, 15g carbs, 1g fiber, 2g sugar, 381mg sodium

Served here with: Quinoa, fresh orange slices, and a salad of micro greens.

"Just a Little Fancy" Salad

This simple, delicious pasta salad has a healthy dose of veggies. The dish is not complex and is, indeed, "just a little fancy." This is a great way to get your kids to eat their veggies because you can throw on more cheese for added incentive. It's wonderful served chilled for a picnic, or warm for a chilly day. I have even enjoyed this on an airplane. It's much better than anything else you can get at 30,000 feet!

Orzo Pasta Salad

Vegetarian

Prep Time 5 minutes
Cook Time 40 minutes
Serves 4

1 cup dry orzo pasta, cooked according to package directions
8 oz Mixed Medley Cherry Tomatoes
1 red onion, diced
1 red bell pepper, diced
1 green bell pepper, diced
1 Tbsp Garlic Olive Oil
Smoked sea salt to taste
Black pepper to taste
2 cups grated cheese (any kind)

1 Preheat oven to 375° F with the rack in the middle. Meanwhile, toss veggies with some garlic oil until they are glistening. Sprinkle with a little smoked sea salt and black pepper. Arrange on a cookie sheet in a single layer. Roast for about 40 minutes until lightly browned and softened.

2 Toss cooked orzo pasta with roasted veggies and top with cheese.

Nutrition Snapshot

Per serving: 344 calories, 9g fat, 4g saturated fat, 16g protein, 50g carbs, 4g fiber, 2g sugar, 179mg sodium

Served here with: Raw sliced broccoli with side of Chunky Olive Hummus and fresh blackberries.

Kelly's Tip!

If you're going on a romantic date, pack this delightful meal and suggest "A Jug of Wine, a Loaf of Bread, and Thou."

Did You Know?

Orzo is the Italian word for barley. Though orzo is shaped like rice and is made from wheat, it was originally made from barley. Confused?

Pack it Yummy!

"One of the very nicest things about life is the way we must regularly stop whatever it is we are doing and devote our attention to eating."
   - Luciano Pavarotti, 'My Own Story'

Astrid Lague

I grew up in rural Vermont, spent a year of high school in rural Sweden, went to college in rural New York state, and later circled back to rural Vermont. I work full-time as a biochemistry research technician, specializing in molecular biology. I also have many hobbies and side projects, including acting, singing, reading, and, of course, cooking and baking.

I was raised to have great passion about cooking healthful, diverse kinds of food. Growing up, I rarely knew what continent would provide the inspiration for the meal my father would prepare. My mother is a bread alchemist, able to make delicious creations from leftover pancake batter, orange juice, cooking liquid from baked beans, and healthy whole grains. It was no surprise that when I started my own family, I began experimenting with food more and more.

When my daughter started school a few years ago, it was only natural that I packed her lunches. We are fortunate to have excellent food in our school district, but I prefer packing her lunches, both for economic reasons and because I like knowing what she is eating. I prefer using reusable containers for my lunches and EasyLunchbox containers simplified lunch packing immensely. When my son, who is a Type 1 Diabetic, started school this past fall, it was even more important to pack his lunches. I know how many grams of carbohydrates I am sending for him to eat. The school nurse, who doses his insulin, can read my blog, Lunches Fit For a Kid (lunchfitforakid.blogspot.com), to know how much insulin he needs for what he eats.

A common refrain heard in my kitchen is, *"I hope you like this, because I kind of made it up."* I think that's apt here.

Rockin' Reuben

Although I had food from all over the world growing up, I don't think I ever had a Reuben until I went to college. I fell in love. They are, in my opinion, pretty close to perfection in a sandwich. They are tangy and flavorful and hit the taste buds in all the right places: sauerkraut, Russian dressing, Swiss cheese, pastrami or corned beef, seedy rye bread. I drool just thinking about them. I talked to my sister, who had also recently discovered Reubens, and she was similarly enamored. Why had we not had these before adulthood? Turns out, our mother doesn't care for sauerkraut, so the beauty of a Reuben is lost on her. I was inspired to mix all of those flavors I love in a Reuben sandwich into a pasta. Thus was born this Reuben Pasta Salad. Enjoy it hot or chilled. I like it both ways, as do my children.

Reuben Pasta Salad

Prep Time 5 minutes
Cook Time 15 minutes
Serves 6

1 lb Vegetable Radiatore Pasta
½ lb uncured corned beef
2 cups Swiss cheese, shredded
1 (14.5-oz) can sauerkraut, drained and rinsed
½ cup Thousand Island dressing
Caraway seeds (optional)

1 Boil pasta according to directions on package. Drain.

2 Chop corned beef into strips. Combine with cheese and sauerkraut. Toss with pasta and stir in dressing.

3 Sprinkle with caraway seeds and serve warm or chilled.

Nutrition Snapshot

Per serving: 521 calories, 20g fat, 8g saturated fat, 23g protein, 61g carbs, 3g fiber, 5g sugar, 880mg sodium

Served here with: Blueberries, grapes, and chunks of kiwi.

Did You Know?

Thousand Island dressing gets its name from the "1,000" islands in the St. Lawrence River between upstate New York (where the dressing was invented) and Canada. It's a variation of Russian dressing, which is also essentially a combination of mayo and ketchup.

Hola Pollo-dilla!

I'm sure I'm not the only one to always end up with leftover chicken from a store-bought rotisserie chicken. One of my favorite things to do with it is to spice it up and repurpose it into something totally lunch-worthy. Anything is better with cheese, and this is no exception. Hooray for quesadillas!

Taco-Spiced Chicken Quesadilla

Prep Time 5 minutes
Cook Time 5 minutes
Serves 4

2 cups cooked rotisserie chicken, shredded
1 tsp Taco Seasoning
¼ cup Red Sauce
8 large whole wheat flour tortillas
1 cup Fancy Shredded Mexican Cheese Blend

1 Combine chicken with taco seasoning and sauce. Spread some of the chicken evenly on a whole wheat tortillas and top with cheese.

2 Put a second tortilla on top, and cook in a skillet on medium-high heat until browned. Flip quesadilla carefully and cook on the other side until it is also browned.

3 Repeat with more tortillas until chicken is used up. Cut into wedges and serve. These are lovely with guacamole, sour cream, and/or salsa. They are also delicious plain. Enjoy!

Nutrition Snapshot
Per serving: 454 calories, 13g fat, 4g saturated fat, 39g protein, 41g carbs, 2g fiber, 0g sugar, 1,077mg sodium

Note: Trader Joe's Taco Seasoning packs a spicy punch. Use sparingly at first and add more to taste. If using other brands of taco seasoning, you will likely use more.

Served here with: Veggie and Flaxseed Tortilla Chips, watermelon strips, guacamole and salsa.

 Kelly's Tip!

Save money on shredded cheese. I buy the five-pound bags of it at the big warehouse store. When I get home, I divide the cheese into four or five quart-size resealable bags. Then I pop those in the freezer. They'll stay fresh for up to six months.

Pack it Yummy!

"One cannot think well, love well, sleep well, if one has not dined well." –Virginia Woolf

Aviva Goldfarb

As the mother of two active teenagers with formerly picky palates, I know the challenge of putting appealing but healthy homemade dinners on the table amidst the chaos of daily life.

Recalling the simple weekly meal-planning strategy that my mom used when we were kids, I developed a system that takes the "scramble" out of the dinner hour. I then took what worked for my own family and founded a dinner planning service, The Six O'Clock Scramble (thescramble.com).

I give thousands of families an easy, online meal-planning and grocery-shopping system, along with fail-proof, family-friendly recipes.

My family dinner cookbooks, *The Six O'Clock Scramble* and *SOS! The Six O'Clock Scramble to the Rescue* debuted in 2006 and 2010. Both the cookbooks and online meal-planning service have won praise from reviewers at O Magazine, Working Mother, USA Today, Real Simple, The Washington Post, and many others. I also love helping parents lure their kids into the kitchen through my weekly posts on PBS Parents Kitchen Explorers.

Over the years, I have grown increasingly concerned with reducing our environmental impact while still enjoying the foods we love. In our family, we buy much of our food locally at farmer's markets; we have reduced the amount of meat we eat and the amount of food we waste; we've started composting; and each day, we pack our kids low-waste or waste-free lunches. We love the simplicity of using EasyLunchbox containers. They make it quicker and easier to get the kids out the door with a homemade meal in their backpacks at a ridiculously early hour. My son Solomon recently said, "Mom, thank you so much for packing us an awesome homemade lunch every day. You should see the disgusting cafeteria food that some of my friends have to eat." That definitely makes the extra effort well worth it!

Lunch in the Mediterranean

When my family traveled in Israel this past June, we were astounded by the endless array of beautiful, healthy and creative salads, even at breakfast. Here I've recreated one of our favorites that we enjoyed at Israel's homegrown version of Starbucks, called Aroma. Cut the tomatoes, cucumbers, and onions into small pieces for the best flavor and presentation.

Israeli Salad

Prep Time 20 minutes
Cook Time 20 minutes (for hard-boiled eggs)
Serves 6

4 eggs
2 cucumbers, peeled and diced into small pieces
1 lb cherry tomatoes or 2 large tomatoes, diced into small pieces
½ red onion, finely diced
½ cup fresh parsley, chopped
2 Tbsp tahini (sesame paste), well stirred (or use hummus if you can't find tahini)
Juice of 1 lemon, about 4 Tbsp
2 tsp Dijon mustard (use wheat/gluten-free if needed)
1 tsp minced garlic (1 clove), or 1 cube frozen Crushed Garlic
2 Tbsp water
2 tsp honey
¼ tsp salt

1 Place eggs in medium saucepan and fill with water to cover eggs by 1 inch. Bring to low boil then turn off heat. Let sit for 17 minutes then drain and fill with ice water. Once cooled, peel eggs.

2 Chop peeled eggs and combine in a medium serving bowl with cucumbers, tomatoes, onions and parsley.

3 In a small bowl or large measuring cup, combine tahini, lemon juice, mustard, garlic, water, honey, and salt. Toss salad with dressing. (You might not need all of the dressing.) You can make the salad and dressing up to 4 hours in advance but don't combine them until you are ready to serve.

Nutrition Snapshot
Per serving: 111 calories, 5g fat, 1g saturated fat, 6g protein, 8g carbs, 2g fiber, 2g sugar, 199mg sodium

Homemade Pita Chips

Prep Time 5 minutes
Cook Time 10 – 12 minutes
Serves 6

2 pita pockets, whole wheat or white
2 Tbsp extra virgin olive oil
½ tsp kosher or sea salt (optional)

1 Preheat oven to 350° F. Cut pita pockets in half, separating tops from bottoms, and cut each piece into about 6 triangular wedges (like a pizza). In a medium bowl, toss pita with olive oil and salt.

2 Lay pita wedges on a large baking sheet and bake for 10 - 12 minutes until they start to brown.

Nutrition Snapshot
Per serving: 66 calories, 5g fat, 1g saturated fat, 1g protein, 6g carbs, 1g fiber, 0g sugar, 212mg sodium

Served here with: Yogurt topped with fruit.

Farmer's Market in a Box

When my husband Andrew and I worked as interns in Washington, DC, we sometimes used our meager wages to treat ourselves to these delicious sandwiches from a nearby deli. (Otherwise, we were eating ramen noodle soup in our cramped office.) I re-created them for a picnic recently, and they were just as good as we remembered. We prefer them without tomatoes, but try them both ways (or even with sliced avocado) for variety.

Veggie Delight Sandwiches

Use Udi's gluten-free bagels

Prep Time 5-10 minutes
Serves 6

6 sesame bagels, or any variety
6 oz vegetable cream cheese, light or regular
½ cucumber, peeled and thinly sliced
4 oz alfalfa sprouts (or use 1 avocado, sliced)
1 tomato, thinly sliced (optional)

1 Slice bagels in half and toast lightly. Spread about 2 Tbsp cream cheese on half of each bagel, and top with a layer of cucumbers, sprouts (or avocado), and tomato. Press top half of each bagel on top, and gently slice sandwiches in half.

2 Wrap sandwiches tightly in foil and keep them cool.

Nutrition Snapshot
Per serving: 318 calories, 11g fat, 5g saturated fat, 10g protein, 45g carbs, 2g fiber, 2g sugar, 442mg sodium

Note: If you have some vegetables that you'd like to use up, you can make your own veggie cream cheese. We usually make ours with chopped carrots, bell peppers, and scallions.

Ambrosia Fruit Salad

Prep Time 10 minutes
Serves 6

2 Tbsp plain nonfat or low-fat yogurt or sour cream
1 tsp lemon juice, preferably freshly squeezed
1 Tbsp honey
6 cups seasonal mixed fruit such as strawberries, blueberries, bananas, grapes and/or melon

1 Combine yogurt or sour cream, lemon juice, and honey in a medium bowl.

2 Add fresh fruit and stir gently.

Nutrition Snapshot
Per serving: 85 calories, 0g fat, 0g saturated fat, 1g protein, 23g carbs, 1g fiber, 13g sugar, 18mg sodium

Served here with: Pop Chips

Did You Know?

The best bagels have a crunchy outside, and soft chewy inside because the dough is first boiled and then baked. This two-step process also gives bagels their distinctive shine. Bagels were probably invented in the 1600s in Poland. There are many theories about the origin of the bagel's doughnut-like shape, one being that they were easy for street vendors to stack on a stick. (The bagel came before doughnuts, so maybe doughnuts should be described as "bagel-shaped.") One final note: while there is a big market for doughnut holes, there appears to be no market for "bagel holes."

Pack it Yummy!

Corey Valley

I'm Corey, proud mother of Big D. and Little D. (known as "Double D" when together). I have worn many hats through the years: high-school teacher, middle-school counselor, stay-at-home mom, and always a foodie. When I'm not in the kitchen, you'll find me jogging, at the Pilates studio, or having dance parties with my girls.

My love for preparing and packing lunches for my family was handed down from my mom. Throughout my school years, she took the time to pack me a lunch with a loving note every single day. To this day, I remember how special and loved this made me feel. When I became a mother, I knew how important this simple gesture of love would be for my girls.

Health is the main drive behind my cooking passion. When I cook and pack lunches for my family, I know what is going into their bodies: real food. This is also one of the many reasons I love shopping at Trader Joe's. I can enjoy shopping, knowing that all of my Trader Joe's goodies are free of artificial flavors, colors, preservatives, genetically modified ingredients, and trans fats. Being a lover of all foods, I really wanted to pass that passion for healthy eating down to my children. When they see me having fun with food and are presented with exciting, colorful meals, they are much more likely to try a variety of foods. EasyLunchboxes and Trader Joe's make this task a cinch. Trader Joe's offers a variety of affordable and healthy food, while EasyLunchboxes provide an easy way to present and pack fun, fresh lunches. A perfect pairing, if you ask me!

I have found great joy in posting step-by-step recipes of new, fun, fresh meals that the whole family can enjoy on my blog, Family Fresh Meals (familyfreshmeals.com).

Double D's Dippers

Double D loves waffles, so our waffle iron is always out. For lunch one day, I wanted to make some homemade pizzas for the girls but had no dough on hand. Since I had already pulled my waffle iron out once again, my creative cooking mind kicked on. I always keep a couple tubes of refrigerated Crescent Rolls on hand, and that dough is similar to pizza dough, right? So why not throw it on the waffle iron with all the fixings for a delicious pizza? Yum!

Waffle Pizzaaaah!

Vegetarian
Omit pepperoni and add additional cheese

Prep Time 15 minutes
Cook Time 15 minutes
Serves 8

2 (8-oz) cans refrigerated Crescent Rolls
8 oz Shredded Lite Three Cheese blend
1 tsp 21 Seasoning Salute
1 (16-oz) jar Pizza Sauce
25 pepperoni slices

1 Preheat waffle iron to medium/high and spray with non-stick cooking spray. Meanwhile, combine cheese and 21 Seasoning Salute and set aside.

2 Unroll first can of dough on a flat working surface. Separate dough crosswise, making two 7 x 6-inch rectangles. Firmly press perforations to seal. Repeat for second can. You should now have four rectangles.

3 Place one piece of dough on waffle iron and sprinkle with half the cheese mixture. Top with layer of pepperoni. For vegetarian option, omit pepperoni, and add more cheese if desired. Top with another piece of dough. Close waffle iron and cook for 2-3 minutes, or until dough is golden and crispy.

4 Repeat with other dough sheets. Cut into triangles and serve with side of Pizza Sauce for dipping.

Nutrition Snapshot

Per serving: 306 calories, 16g fat, 9g saturated fat, 11g protein, 30g carbs, 2g fiber, 9g sugar, 428mg sodium

Served here with: Fresh fruit (apples and grapes) and All Butter Shortbread Cookies with Apricot and Raspberry Filling.

Did You Know?

The original ice cream cone was actually a waffle. In 1904 at the St. Louis World's Fair, the ice cream booth ran out of dishes. It was a hot day, and they couldn't wash them fast enough to keep up with the demand. So the man in the waffle booth next door invented something yummier to hold the scoops.

Protein-Packed Lunch

I am always looking for protein-packed lunches that are healthy and will leave me feeling full. These little meat cups are so versatile that you can use them for a variety of occasions. You can serve these cups of joy on a salad as shown here, or as an amazing appetizer at your next party. Simply make the cups and filling ahead of time, refrigerate, and pull out when ready to use. In the side compartment of this EasyLunchbox lunch is the sweet, protein-packed dessert that will leave you and your sweet tooth satisfied. These Gooey Chocolate Nut Bars are a cinch to whip up in no time at all.

Cheesy Prosciutto Cups Over Greens

Gluten Free

Prep Time 25 min
Cook Time 10-15 minutes
Makes 24 prosciutto cups

6 oz sliced prosciutto (about 12 slices)
3 oz heavy whipping cream
4 oz silver goat chevre, or your favorite soft goat cheese
4 oz cream cheese
1 Tbsp minced parsley
1 tsp minced basil
Mixed greens

1 Preheat oven to 375° F.

2 Cut each prosciutto slice down the middle to make thinner strips. Lay each prosciutto half-slice inside a 24-cup mini muffin pan. Overlap sides to make a meat cup. Bake for 9-10 minutes. Remove from oven and allow to cool for a couple minutes. After cooled, place on paper towel to drain off any excess grease.

3 Place whipping cream, goat cheese, cream cheese, and herbs into a mixing bowl; beat until thick and creamy. Put cheese mixture into a piping bag. If you don't have one, just use a large zip-lock bag and cut off a corner to pipe with. Pipe whipped cheese mixture into each cup and serve on a bed of mixed greens.

Nutrition Snapshot
Per meat cup: 50 calories, 4g fat, 2g saturated fat, 3g protein, 1g carbs, 0g fiber, 0g sugar, 224mg sodium

Gooey Chocolate Nut Bars

Vegetarian

Prep Time 25
Cook Time 25 minutes (with refrigeration, ready in about 2 hours 30 minutes)
Makes 24 bars

1 (8-oz) can refrigerated Crescent Rolls
1 cup white chocolate chips
1 ½ cups semisweet chocolate chips
1 ¼ cup sliced almonds
1 ¼ cup whole cashews
1 (14-oz) bottle sweetened condensed milk

1 Heat oven to 350° F. Unroll dough into 2 rectangles. Spray a 9 x 13-inch pan with nonstick cooking spray. Place your 2 rectangles of dough in pan and press over the bottom and slightly up the sides. Bake for 4-6 minutes.

2 Remove partially baked crust from oven.

3 (With adult supervision, now would be the perfect time to have the kiddos help out!) Sprinkle with white chocolate chips, then chocolate chips. Next sprinkle on almonds. Finally, sprinkle cashews evenly over crust. Pour sweetened condensed milk evenly over the top.

4 Bake 20 to 25 minutes longer or until golden brown. Let cool for about 20 minutes and then run a spatula around edges of pan to loosen crust and to prevent sticking. Chill in refrigerator for 2-3 hours or until chocolate is set.

Nutrition Snapshot
Per bar: 314 calories, 16g fat, 4g saturated fat, 20g protein, 37g carbs, 2g fiber, 30g sugar, 106mg sodium

Served here with: Fresh strawberries and blueberries.

Kelly's Tip! Instead of an ice block, place a frozen juice box or water bottle in the lunch bag. It will keep the food chilled, and by lunchtime the juice will have thawed. Put the frozen drink or ice block in a clean sock to absorb condensation if there is too much moisture. (This occurs more often in humid climates.)

Pack it Yummy!

"In spite of food fads, fitness programs, and health concerns, we must never lose sight of a beautifully conceived meal." – Julia Child

Emily Trenbeath

I'm Emily, and I strive to present healthy foods to my young children in ways that interest them and get them to be more adventurous in their tastes. It seems I'm succeeding, because my older daughter eats more fruits, vegetables (raw and cooked), and ethnic foods than most other children I know. I take new foods, cut them into interesting shapes, and decorate them. Then I pack it all into an adorable bento box.

While I live in Atlanta now, I'm a Maryland girl at heart, having been born and raised in the Annapolis area. My father is an Englishman and my mother grew up in a Navy family, traveling to places like Korea, Japan, Morocco, and Cyprus. Thus, I was raised with a fantastically wide range of international cuisines, which I want to share with my children.

I learned to cook at my mother's elbow. She is a phenomenal cook and baker who used to grind wheat berries into flour, make the most mouth-watering bread, and sell it in small, handmade batches. She, in turn, learned from her mother, who was famous in Navy circles for putting on elaborate dinners for international dignitaries. From my paternal grandmother, I learned the value of food conservation, and of using what you have on hand to make meals and make do. Living in England, she survived years of rationing through both World Wars, as did my father in early childhood. Let me tell you, nothing went to waste, for better or for worse! I work part-time, mostly from home, as an IT manager, freelance copywriter, and voice-recording professional. I blog, sharing my adventures with lunches, munchies, and bentos on Bentobloggy (bentobloggy.com). I also collect pretty aprons, vintage Descoware (Cherry-Flame) and Le Creuset (Flame) enameled cast-iron pieces, so if you see anything neat, drop me a line!

My philosophy: Don't just assume your kid won't eat it. You will never know if you don't offer it.

Vampire Beware Taters and Sausage!

These garlicky potatoes are one of my favorite go-to meals, and they work for lunch, too. I combine crispy garlic potatoes in Parmesan sauce, and sauté them with sliced Italian chicken sausage. Because my whole family loves them so much, I make sure to always have a bag of these in my freezer, so I can pull them out at a moment's notice. As a bonus, your entire kitchen will smell divine!

Garlic Potatoes & Chicken Sausage

Prep Time 5 min
Cook Time 10 minutes
Serves 4

1 (16-oz) pkg frozen Garlic Potatoes with Parmesan Sauce
1 (10-oz) pkg Italian Chicken Sausage, or 6 links of other sausage, sliced diagonally
2 Tbsp olive oil

1 Sauté potatoes and sausage in olive oil until browned and crispy.

Nutrition Snapshot

Per serving: 497 calories, 20g fat, 5g saturated fat, 24g protein, 46g carbs, 0g fiber, 2g sugar, 1,305mg sodium

Served here with: Spinach salad with Ranch dressing, sliced strawberries.

Kelly's Tip!

If you eat garlic while on a date, make sure you BOTH eat it, unless you're dating a vampire.

Did You Know?

Garlic is a natural disinfectant known to kill 23 different kinds of bacteria. It's also a natural insect repellent against blood-sucking mosquitoes, which may be the origin of the story that it keeps away blood-sucking vampires.

Pizza Adventure

My daughter loves to help me make these. She feels like an adventurous chef and is more likely to try special toppings, like prosciutto instead of deli ham. Be creative and have fun with it. This recipe makes one naan pizza, nice for a hearty snack, or a good-sized kid lunch.

Naan Ham Pizza

Prep Time 5 min
Cook Time 9-10 min
Serves 1

1 piece Naan Bread
2 Tbsp Bruschetta sauce (fresh or jarred, or marinara)
2 Tbsp shredded mozzarella cheese
1 slice ham, 3 slices salami, or 6 slices pepperoni (diced as desired)

1   Preheat oven to 400° F. Place naan on baking sheet and add sauce, mozzarella, and your choice of ham/salami/pepperoni. Bake for 9-10 minutes.

Nutrition Snapshot
Per serving: 507 calories, 28g fat, 10g saturated fat, 24g protein, 40g carbs, 3g fiber, 1g sugar, 825mg sodium

Served here with: Pineapple chunks, red and green bell pepper.

Pack it Yummy!

Lisa Leake

I am a wife, mother, foodie, and blogger who chronicles my family's journey as we seek out the real food in our processed-food world. I've always loved to cook and prepare meals for others, but at the beginning of 2010 I suddenly realized I had no idea where our food came from. I'd never before read an ingredient label, never been to a farmer's market, and never purchased anything that was organic, at least not on purpose. Thanks to a book by Michael Pollan and the documentary, *Food, Inc.*, I was given the wake-up call of my life. I knew it was time for some serious changes. The transition wasn't easy at first, but we slowly revamped everything – from what we bought, to where we shopped, to how we cooked. From there my mission to cut out processed food and my blog, 100 Days of Real Food (100daysofrealfood.com), began.

"I like it when my mommy makes the recipes I pick out of the cookbook." - Sydney, age 7.

"It's not food if it arrived through the window of your car." – Michael Pollan

Summer in a Box

Few dishes say summer to me more than Caprese salad. I love this dish because it's packed with lots of fresh flavor, but it might also be one of my favorite salads because there's no lettuce involved. Plus it's super quick and easy to throw together. You can make homemade pesto yourself or, if you like shortcuts, pick up a small tub of pre-made pesto from Trader Joe's. Either way, you'll end up with a filling, flavorful, unprocessed lunch.

Caprese Heaven

Prep Time 5 minutes
Cook Time None
Serves 2

1 cup Ciliegine Whole Milk Fresh Mozzarella balls
1 cup sugar plum tomatoes, sliced in half
2 Tbsp refrigerated Genova Pesto
Pinch salt
Black pepper to taste

1 In large compartment, mix together mozzarella balls, tomatoes, and pesto.

2 Season with salt and pepper.

Nutrition Snapshot
Per serving: 207 calories, 16g fat, 6g saturated fat, 14g protein, 6g carbs, 1g fiber, 3g sugar, 97mg sodium

Pine Nut Quinoa

Prep Time 5 minutes
Cook Time 2 minutes
Serves 1

½ cup cooked Organic Tricolor Quinoa or regular quinoa
1 tsp extra virgin olive oil
1 Tbsp pine nuts
Pinch salt

1 In a small sauté pan heat olive oil over medium-low heat. Once oil is warm, toss in pine nuts and stir frequently until nuts are lightly brown, about 1–2 minutes.

2 Remove from heat immediately and mix with cooked quinoa and salt. Can be eaten cold or reheated.

Nutrition Snapshot
Per serving: 258 calories, 13g fat, 1g saturated fat, 7g protein, 31g carbs, 3g fiber, 3g sugar, 143 mg mg sodium

Served here with: Steamed asparagus.

 **Kelly's Tip!** Flatten your cooler bag and put it in the freezer to chill before loading your lunch. It will stay cool even longer.

Asian Influence

It's hard to go wrong when soy sauce is involved. Leave boring sandwiches behind and switch it up with this portable, filling lunch that contains nothing but fresh whole foods.

"Daddy, did you make that? It looks so good, it looks like mommy made it." -Sienna, age 5

Un-Fried Rice

Vegetarian
Gluten Free

Use tamari or gluten-free soy sauce

Prep Time 5 minutes
Cook Time None
Serves 2

1 ¼ cups cooked brown basmati rice, or frozen fully cooked brown rice
Half an avocado, diced
¼ cup Ready-to-Eat Shelled Edamame Soybeans
1 ½ Tbsp soy sauce

1   Add cooked rice to large compartment and stir in avocado, edamame, and soy sauce. Can be eaten cold or reheated.

Nutrition Snapshot
Per serving: 271 calories, 10g fat, 1g saturated fat, 7g protein, 36g carbs, 6g fiber, 1g sugar, 462mg sodium

Served here with: Diced fresh pineapple and Roasted Cashews.

Did You Know?

Brown rice has only the outermost layer – the husk – removed. It has nutrients not found in white rice, which is produced when the bran layer and germ layer are also removed. Brown rice has vitamin B1, vitamin B3, iron, magnesium, fiber, and bran oil, which may help lower LDL cholesterol.

Lucky Leftovers

We practically fight over leftovers in our house, and this quiche is no exception. It's great either cold or reheated, and can be made with whatever fillings your heart desires. Plus, the homemade whole-wheat crust combined with fresh ingredients means this is yet another simple "real food" lunch dish.

Homemade Quiche with Easy Whole-Wheat Crust

Vegetarian

Prep Time 10-15 minutes
Cook Time 30-40 minutes
Serves 6

Crust
½ cups whole wheat flour
½ cup unsalted butter, melted
½ tsp salt
2 Tbsp milk

Filling
4 eggs
1 ½ cups milk or half-and-half
Salt and cayenne pepper, to taste
²/₃ cup optional ingredients: shredded cheddar, diced ham, chopped cooked veggies, goat cheese, sautéed mushrooms, caramelized onions, Swiss cheese, or cooked bacon

1 Preheat oven to 375° F. Meanwhile, in a 9-inch pie pan, combine crust ingredients and mix with a fork. Using your hands, form dough into a ball and press down into pan, flattening into an even layer. Bring crust up on the sides and pinch the top perimeter with your finger or a fork. Set aside raw crust.

2 In a large bowl, whisk together eggs, milk , salt, and cayenne. Stir in desired optional ingredients and pour mixture into crust. Bake for 30-40 minutes or until eggs are set and top is slightly brown.

Nutrition Snapshot
Per serving: 351 calories, 22g fat, 12g saturated fat, 13g protein, 26g carbs, 4g fiber, 3g sugar, 371mg sodium

Served here with: Fresh strawberries and blueberries, 1 Cashew Cookie Lara Bar (unwrapped and broken in half).

Did You Know?

Though we think of quiche as a cheese pie these days, the original Quiche Lorraine did not contain cheese. It had only eggs, custard, and meat. When the dish evolved into a cheesy vegetarian dish, the phrase "real men don't eat quiche" became popular.

 **Kelly's Tip!**

Save the leftover scraps of food that accumulate while cutting decorative shapes from meats, cheese, and veggies for your lunches. They can make a handy and tasty addition to a quiche or omelet recipe.

Pack it Yummy!

Anna and Ben, learning how to manage their food allergies, pack lunch with Mclanie

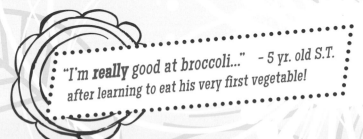

"I'm **really** good at broccoli..." - 5 yr. old S.T. after learning to eat his very first vegetable!

Melanie Potock

I have the best job ever: I'm a feeding specialist! My job is to teach children to be more adventurous eaters and learn the joy of food. I work with a variety of little munch bugs; from children with special needs, to those with food allergies or food sensitivities, to the garden-variety picky eater. In working with children who have difficulty eating in various environments, I often visit kids in their school cafeterias – otherwise known as the school CAFÉ-FEARIA, according to one 7-year-old client of mine. Even the dynamics of the school cafeteria can make or break a nutritious lunch. I know the importance of kids being involved in the kitchen, as well as in the lunch-packing process.

I am the mother of two daughters, now in their early 20s. Raising a family that included one particularly picky eater taught me that learning to be an adventurous eater is a gradual process, so you might as well enjoy the journey. My love for kids and food is what drives me. That's why the My Munch Bug motto is "for the love of food!"

Melanie Potock, MA, CCC-SLP is a certified speech language pathologist, a national speaker on the topic of picky eating, the author of Happy Mealtimes with Happy Kids, and the executive producer of the acclaimed children's music CD, Dancing in the Kitchen: Songs that Celebrate the Joy of Food. EasyLunchboxes are her first choice for kids in the school cafeteria, where easy-open lids are essential so healthy, nutritious foods can be within easy reach. Melanie's website, My Munch Bug (mymunchbug.com), offers tips for a variety of kids, including those with food allergies.

Power-Packed Quinoa

Wonder how to find the protein, vitamin E, niacin and other nutrients found in nuts when you have a nut allergy? Here's a recipe that fits the bill. Protein packed quinoa is boosted with chia seeds (more protein plus omega 3 fatty acids and fiber), dried apricots (vitamin E and niacin), spinach (iron), and crunchy sunflower seeds (vitamin B1, B6, and folate). A side dish of garlicky roasted chickpeas adds a final punch of protein, as well as iron, calcium, and fiber. Add fresh orange slices bursting with vitamin C to aid in iron absorption, and this power-packed lunch will see you through the rest of the day!

Quinoa with Chia, Apricots, and Sunflower Seeds

Vegetarian
Use vegetable stock

Gluten Free
Choose gluten-free broth

Prep Time 30 min
Cook Time 20 min
Serves 4

2 cups uncooked Tri Color Quinoa or use regular quinoa
4 cups organic chicken broth or vegetable stock
1 cup coarsely chopped dried apricots
6 Tbsp organic chia seeds (check package to ensure
   no cross contamination in facility)
2 Tbsp extra virgin olive oil
2 Tbsp rice vinegar
2 Tbsp lemon juice
4 Tbsp minced purple onion
2 cups loosely packed fresh spinach leaves
¾ cup sunflower seed kernels (raw or roasted)

1 Cook quinoa according to package directions, using broth instead of water. Add apricots and quinoa to the broth at the same time. Just before all liquid is absorbed, stir in chia seeds.

2 Fluff with fork and allow to cool.

3 Whisk together olive oil, vinegar, and lemon juice in a small bowl and add slowly to quinoa to moisten.

4 Chop spinach into bite-size pieces. Stir in onion, spinach, and sunflower seeds. Best served chilled.

Nutrition Snapshot
Per serving: 713 calories, 31g fat, 2g saturated fat, 25g protein, 99g carbs, 19g fiber, 24g sugar, 93mg sodium

Garlicky Roasted Chickpeas

Vegetarian
Gluten Free

Prep Time 5 minutes
Cook Time 30-45 minutes
Serves 2

1 (15-oz) can chickpeas (garbanzo beans)
1 Tbsp garlic salt (or more if you like a little more kick!)
2 Tbsp olive oil

1   Preheat oven to 400° F. Rinse chickpeas thoroughly until no foam appears. Pat dry with a paper towel. If skins slide off peas, discard skins. Toss chickpeas, olive oil, and garlic salt gently in a bowl.

2   Spread chickpeas on cookie sheet and roast for 30 to 45 minutes until golden brown with a slight crunch. Cool.

Nutrition Snapshot
Per serving: 299 calories, 15g fat, 2g saturated fat, 9g protein, 33g carbs, 9g fiber, 2g sugar, 1,050mg sodium

Served here with: Orange slices

Kelly's Tip!

Quinoa is cooked to perfection when you can see a little curled "tail" springing from each grain.

Did You Know?

Quinoa (which can be pronounced either "keenowa" or "keenwa") looks like a grain but is actually the seed of a vegetable related to spinach and Swiss chard.

South of the Border Bowl

This zesty, speedy lunch is packed in a snap. The combination of rice, protein-rich black beans, fire roasted corn, and your favorite TJ's salsa adds just the right zing. Serve this fiesta of yumminess with a side of guacamole and TJ's Veggie and Flaxseed Tortilla Chips for a burst of omega 3 fatty acids. Muy delicioso!

Corn, Beans, and Rice Bowl

Vegetarian
Gluten Free

Prep Time 30 minutes (includes time to allow rice to cool)
Cook Time 3 minutes for rice/microwave
Serves 4

2 (10-oz) pouches (4 cups) frozen brown rice, prepared according to package directions
1 (15-oz) can black beans, rinsed (until no foam appears) and drained
1 cup frozen Fire Roasted Corn, thawed
¼ cup Fancy Shredded Mexican Cheese Blend
3 lime wedges
2 sprigs fresh cilantro

1 Cool rice to room temperature, then fold in beans and corn. Gently fold in cheese last.

2 Garnish with 2 lime wedges and cilantro once transferred to EasyLunchbox container. (Squeeze a third lime wedge over guacamole to maintain color and add a little bit of zip! Garnish with cilantro.)

Nutrition Snapshot
Per serving: 358 calories, 3g fat, 1g saturated fat, 14g protein, 68g carbs, 10g fiber, 4g sugar, 428mg sodium

Served here with: Guacamole, sprinkled with lime juice to maintain color and garnished with cilantro. Veggie and Flaxseed Tortilla Chips and a side of salsa.

 **Kelly's Tip!**

Eat rice and beans together because they form a complete protein. Meat and dairy have all the essential amino acids that are needed to keep your body running properly, but if you are a vegetarian (or just want a break from bacon and eggs) you can create the same effect by eating rice and beans in the same meal.

Pack it For Work!

A taste of home, right at your desk

Do you buy lunch every day while you're on the job? Add up how much it's costing you. You may be surprised. Instead of heading to the cafeteria, drive-thru, or a restaurant, bring your lunch to work. Your savings (and your satisfaction) will add up. (But no working while eating, okay? They don't call it a lunch "break" for nothing!)

THE MASCIULLO FAMILY
DAN, KAREN, TOMMY & MOLLY

Tortilla Pizza

- Hand-made Tortilla
- 3-Cheese Blend
- Marinara
- Red Peppers
- Olives
- Cornmeal

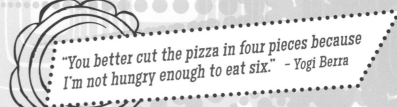

"You better cut the pizza in four pieces because I'm not hungry enough to eat six." - Yogi Berra

Dan Masciullo

In the fall of 1998, while still in my late 20s, I set out east from the picturesque foothills of Northwest Montana in search of prospective in-laws who would initiate and arrange a blind date with their only daughter. She would, in turn, accept, which would mean driving 180 miles every other weekend to engage in a yearlong dating ritual that would culminate in a televised marriage proposal on a local Peoria news station. My goal was lofty, but I achieved it by 2003.

My lovely wife Karen and I now live in the suburbs of Chicago with our two children, Tommy and Molly. I provide consulting services in the eCommerce industry, and Karen leverages the organizational and disciplinary skills she gained during her 9-year tenure as a kindergarten teacher in her current position as a professional mom. Our family is active, we have a keen interest in health and nutrition, and we like long moonlit walks on the beach. I wouldn't classify myself as a gourmet chef, but I would classify myself as a gourmet eater. I'm not picky, but my taste buds know good food when they meet it. I like to think that others would appreciate the same kinds of food I myself enjoy.

You can find me messing around on my experimental blog, Trending Healthy (TrendingHealthy.com).

Pizza Gone Viral

I love pizza. I could eat it for breakfast, lunch, and dinner. With this simple, quick recipe, you can have a no-holds-barred full-on lunch battle with the best of them. This quick and tasty pizza was born of an empty pantry and a ravenous appetite. I made it to thank an out-of-town friend for helping me fix a leak in my roof. He asked for the recipe, so I went a step further and posted a video of me making the pizza. With no promotion, the video ("Tortilla Pizza Tutorial" on YouTube) has now been viewed by thousands of people from all around the world.

If you like to breathe air, you might really enjoy this tasty treat that has become an absolute staple in my household, and the go-to meal for a sure-fire way to impress friends and houseguests.

Tortilla Pizza

Vegetarian
Choose vegetarian toppings

Prep Time 10 minutes
Cook Time 6 minutes
Serves 2

1 (8-inch) flour tortilla
1 tsp water
1 Tbsp yellow cornmeal
4 Tbsp Organic Marinara Sauce
½ cup Shredded 3 Cheese Blend (mozzarella, jack, cheddar)
1 Tbsp chopped green onion
1 Tbsp chopped red pepper
1 Tbsp cubed ham or any other pizza fixins you like
½ cup fresh veggie mix (celery, carrots, cucumbers, etc.)
4 Tbsp Ranch Dressing

1 Preheat oven to 485 °F. If using a pizza stone, leave stone in oven while oven preheats. Meanwhile pour 1 tsp water in center of tortilla, then use fingers or a basting brush to coat entire side of tortilla. Sprinkle cornmeal on wet side of tortilla. Place tortilla on baking sheet, cornmeal-side down.

2 Evenly cover dry side of tortilla with marinara sauce, starting from center of tortilla and working all the way out to the edges. Sprinkle cheese, green onion, red pepper, and ham evenly over tortilla.

3 Transfer tortilla directly to pizza stone, or if using baking sheet, place in oven on center rack. Bake for 6 minutes.

4 Remove pizza from oven and slice into 4 equal pieces.

Stack pieces on top of each other with a piece of dry-wax paper separating each piece. Place stacked pieces into large compartment.

Nutrition Snapshot
Per serving: 184 calories, 6g fat, 3g saturated fat, 12g protein, 19g carbs, 1g fiber, 1g sugar, 391mg sodium

Served here with: Fresh veggie mix and veggie dip.

Did You Know?

Pizza was originally a Greek/Mediterranean dish for the poor and working class. It evolved into the Italian version we recognize today in the city of Naples, where it became popular among both the lower and upper classes.

Pack it For Work!

"Ask not what you can do for your country. Ask what's for lunch."
– Orson Welles

Doug Fitzsimmons

I grew up in Arizona in a family where the men rarely cooked. I left the state for college, taking with me a love of fine dining, but no knowledge of cooking. During my sophomore year, a dorm-mate and I transformed his room into a high-class restaurant, Café à la Rick's Place, to invite a couple of female students to dinner. The local gourmet grocer in town helped me with the recipe for tequila-roasted duck, served with rice topped with honey-braised peaches. And right then, I was hooked on cooking.

Cooking skills helped me outside the kitchen, too. When I met my wife Lauri's parents, I cooked for them in order to make a good impression. I made a pan-seared boneless chicken breast with toasted almonds and a port cream sauce. I started the meal with a two-color melon chilled soup (honeydew with mint on one side and cantaloupe with lemon on the other). And right then, they were hooked on me!

Now Lauri and I cook together. Our son Patrick is never far from the kitchen.

"One of our favorite things to do as a family is our monthly organized trip to the park with our church to feed the homeless. I love that Doug always puts a great deal of time and effort into creating gourmet meals for us to share with them." – Lauri Fitzsimmons, proud wife to Doug

Cow on a Cloud

I love to experiment with making tasty burgers. Who doesn't love a good burger? We wanted one before we went to see our dear friend in a play. (Hmm, who was that again? Oh yes, Kelly Lester!) So we stopped in for a burger at the Bowery in Hollywood. My wife couldn't stop laughing because I was making rather audible yummy noises with each bite. Here's my attempt to create a burger that would rival that absolute monument to deliciousness. I left off the bun so my gluten-sensitive wife could enjoy it too!

Angus Beef Burger on a Bed of Mashed Potatoes

Gluten Free

Prep Time 10 minutes
Cook Time 10 minutes
Serves 4

1 lb ground beef, such as Butcher Shop 80/20
1 oz California Mild Cheddar Cheese cut into twelve ¼-inch cubes
1 cube frozen chopped basil
¼ tsp salt
¼ tsp black pepper
1 Tbsp extra virgin olive oil
1 (28-oz) pkg Frozen Mashed Potatoes

1. Microwave frozen basil for 10 seconds. Combine basil with ground beef, salt, and pepper; knead to combine. Form 4 balls with ground beef mixture. Incorporate 3 cubes of cheese into each ball of beef (cheese should not be visible on surface of beef, once incorporated.) Form each ball into a patty, with the center slightly indented.

2. Heat olive oil in cast iron skillet on high. Add patties to skillet and sear for approximately 4 minutes each side, taking care not to burn. Remove from heat.

3. Microwave each patty separately for 1 minute to cook center to a medium rare. (Reheating patty will result in a medium burger.)

4. Prepare frozen mashed potatoes per directions on label.

Place mashed potatoes in main compartment, and place Angus burger patty on top of mashed potatoes. Reheat in EasyLunchboxes for 60 seconds when ready to serve.

Nutrition Snapshot
Per serving: 525 calories, 32g fat, 14g saturated fat, 24g protein, 35g carbs, 4g fiber, 2g sugar, 809mg sodium

Served here with: Sliced strawberries and Pita Chips.

Kelly's Tip!
Impress people at cocktail parties with the word "pareidolia." It's when your brain makes you see or hear something familiar that really isn't there. For example, clouds shaped like animals, the man in the moon, and records played backwards that have hidden messages. Pareidolia has occurred in our house: I once made my daughter Julia a breakfast that included a mini bagel with cream cheese on a small plate. She said, "Mom, is that supposed to be a happy face?" Umm, no Julia. That would be a bagel that broke into a few pieces while I was pulling it apart. It was thanks to my friend Irene McDermott, a very smart librarian, that I learned Julia had experienced pareidolia as a result of my culinary skills. Or lack thereof.

All Thai'd Up at the Office

As a busy attorney, I get so caught up in depositions and court trials that sometimes I don't have time to go out and grab a healthy meal. I love packing this for those times I know I'll be tied up at the office. It's something that will keep me going until I can get home to my family.

Chicken With Lemon Pasta

Prep Time 5 minutes
Cook Time 20 minutes
Serves 4

1 (8-oz) pkg Lemon Pepper Pappardelle Pasta
4 boneless and skinless chicken thighs
½ cup Shredded Carrots (available pre-shredded)
½ cup frozen Fire Roasted Bell Peppers and Onions, thawed
2 Tbsp extra virgin olive oil, divided
¼ cup Thai Lime and Chile Cashews broken into pieces
2 Tbsp Sweet Chili Sauce
1 Tbsp chopped fresh cilantro

1 Cook pasta according to package directions; drain and set aside. Meanwhile, cut chicken into large bite-size pieces.

2 Heat 1 Tbsp olive oil in skillet on high heat. Add chicken and cook until browned, approximately 4 minutes. Remove from heat and set aside.

3 Add 1 Tbsp olive oil to heated skillet and add carrots and Fire Roasted Bell Peppers and Onions. Cook until tender, approximately 3 minutes. Add cooked pasta and chicken; mix thoroughly. Add in cashews and chili sauce and heat, stirring frequently to mix. Top with fresh, chopped cilantro.

Place in large compartment of EasyLunchbox. Remove muffin cups from smaller compartments to reheat when ready to serve.

Nutrition Snapshot
Per serving: 320 calories, 9g fat, 1g saturated fat, 24g protein, 34g carbs, 3g fiber, 4g sugar, 124mg sodium

Served here with: Green grapes and Savory Oriental Rice Crackers in removable muffin cups.

Kelly's Tip! Taking soup or a hot dish with your lunch container? Fill a thermos with boiling water to heat the core for a few minutes. Pour out the water just before you fill the thermos with soup or your entrée. The thermos is heated and ready for your hot food, and will stay that way longer. When I pack a thermos, I put the ice block in the bottom of the cooler, the container on top of the ice block to keep it cool, and the thermos on top, away from the ice.

Thailand was known as "Siam" until 1939. Though Siamese culture is hundreds of years old, the famous noodle dish Pad Thai has only been popular in Thailand since World War II.

Sock It to Me Salmon

I like my food spicy hot, like "make your eyeballs sweat" hot. I toned down this recipe for the faint of heart, but feel free to amp up the heat. The Food Network taught me to cook salmon on the grill using a cedar plank. You can also bake it in the oven during those cold winter months to get your "heat" on!

Cedar-Plank Grilled Salmon

Prep Time 50 minutes
Cook Time 15 minutes
Serves 4

Gluten Free

1 cedar grilling plank
4 (6-oz) fillets Sockeye Salmon, thawed if frozen
¼ tsp cayenne pepper
4 heaping Tbsp Organic Superfruit Spread
1 cup cooked jasmine or brown rice
1 Tbsp extra virgin olive oil

1 Soak cedar plank fully submerged in water for 40 minutes. (Cedar plank may start to smoke heavily if heat is too high so have a spray bottle of water handy when grilling.)

2 Preheat outdoor grill on low setting or 300° F. Place soaked cedar plank on top of heated grill. Rub each fillet to coat with olive oil and place skin side down on top of cedar planks. Sprinkle each fillet with cayenne pepper. Top each fillet with Superfruit Spread and spread evenly. Cook for approximately 15 minutes, checking occasionally for doneness (when no longer translucent in center).

3 Remove from heat and serve over ¼ cup rice.

Nutrition Snapshot
Per serving: 425 calories, 19g fat, 3g saturated fat, 38g protein, 26g carbs, 1g fiber, 8g sugar, 83mg sodium

Served here with: Seasoned Brussels Sprouts made according to package directions and Dark Chocolate Nutty Bits in removable muffin cup (remove before reheating).

 **Kelly's Tip!**

Super useful gift idea: One of the best wedding gifts we received was an inexpensive rice cooker. I've used it practically every week for over two decades. (If the relatives who gave us beautiful vases or china for our wedding are reading this, of course we loved your gifts too!)

Pack it For Work!

"One should eat to live, not live to eat." - Moliere

Kristie Winget

I taught myself to cook, and I have always loved cooking for my family: Eight years ago, my youngest son had to go on a gluten-free and casein-free diet. I had never even heard of gluten or casein, but I took on this new cooking challenge with a positive attitude and learned all I could. I was surprised to find that I am also gluten-intolerant.

Once I realized how important eating the right foods were to my son's well-being and mine, I began to wonder what would happen if I could feed the rest of our family higher quality nutritious food. I love a cooking challenge, and once again I learned all I could. I have since developed a fearless attitude toward cooking. I can make healthy food more fun to eat than junk food. I can make any dish gluten-free or more nutritious. I now prefer to feed my family food that is in its most natural state possible.

I believe in eating five small meals a day, so packing lunches and snacks is a way of life for me. When I discovered the Japanese art of creating bento lunches, I knew right away it was for me. I am in my element when packing a great lunch box. I show my family I love them by making nutritious and fun lunches packed artfully whenever I can. My family consists of me and my husband Rusty, our son Collin and his wife Alicia, our daughter Channing, and our sons Cameron and Sam. I'm very lucky that they are willing taste-testers and my biggest food fans! I write about my healthy lunch packing adventures in my blog, Beneficial Bento (beneficial-bento.com).

"Kristie is one of the most creative people I know, and she is always finding new ways to express her talent. Her first priority is taking care of her family, and when she discovered bento lunches and 'lovely' lunches in general, it was a perfect tool for her. Kristie makes my lunches every day, and I have been so proud of how artistic (not to mention delicious) they are that I started taking pictures of them and posting them on Facebook. Everyone loves seeing what I post and always comments on how clever the ideas are. Our family is fortunate that Kristie wants to be a stay-at-home mom. Even though I am the one that earns the living, Kristie is the one who makes life worth living. Everything she makes, she makes with love. Anyone who knows her will tell you that. That's the secret ingredient in everything she creates."
- Rusty Winget, proud husband to Kristie

Hands Down Favorite Sandwich

When our family is going somewhere and we need to pack a picnic or lunches, this sandwich is everyone's favorite, hands down. The pesto cream cheese is the obvious star of this sandwich, but the combination of grilled chicken, savory turkey bacon, lettuce, and tomato make it complete. I like to make a double batch of the pesto cream cheese. It keeps well in the fridge and is the foundation for lots of good sandwiches (that is, if I can keep my family from using it up as a dip for crackers, chips, and veggies).

"When I heard my mom was going to be testing her bento lunch recipes on us, I wasn't particularly excited. I thought I'd be taking a cute lunch, fit for a 5-year-old, to high school for a couple of weeks. So I was pleasantly surprised when I opened my lunch box and found her amazing cream cheese pesto BLT. The food looks good in pictures, but it tastes even better." - Cameron Winget, Kristie's son

Chicken BLT with Pesto Cream Cheese

Gluten Free

Use gluten-free bread

Prep Time 20 minutes
Cook Time 20 minutes
Serves 4

2 boneless, skinless chicken breasts
8 slices sourdough, whole wheat, or other hearty whole grain bread
Pesto Cream Cheese (recipe below)
8 slices turkey bacon, cooked until crisp
4 slices tomato
Leafy lettuce, such as romaine or spinach
Pinch salt
Pinch black pepper

1   Season chicken with salt and pepper. Grill or pan fry until cooked through. Cool slightly and cut each breast lengthwise so there are 4 large, thin slices of chicken.

2   Toast bread. Spread each slice generously with Pesto Cream Cheese. Top with lettuce, tomato, bacon, and chicken. Put sandwich together and cut in half.

Pesto Cream Cheese

4 oz reduced fat cream cheese
4 large fresh basil leaves
¼ cup chopped spinach leaves, either fresh, or frozen and thawed
½ tsp garlic powder
⅓ cup grated Parmesan and Romano cheese
1 tsp balsamic vinegar

1   Blend all ingredients in a food processor or mini chopper until smooth and creamy.

Nutrition Snapshot
Per sandwich: 369 calories, 11g fat, 5g saturated fat, 37g protein, 30g carbs, 2g fiber, 0g sugar, 948mg sodium

Served here with: Coleslaw and Ridge Cut Sweet Potato Chips.

Kelly's Tip! Make your own quickie coleslaw using bagged Broccoli Slaw mixed with plain Greek yogurt and a little Dijon mustard.

Husband-Tested Chicken

My husband loves feta cheese, so I make this recipe frequently for him. When I do, he tells our kids it tastes terrible just so they won't eat any and he'll have the leftovers for lunch the next day. One of these days, they'll try it and maybe I'll have to start making a double batch.

Greek Chicken

Prep Time 5 minutes
Cook Time 20 minutes
Serves 6

6 boneless, skinless chicken breasts
¼ cup olive oil
Juice from 1 lemon
1 clove garlic, crushed, or 1 cube frozen Crushed Garlic, thawed
3 cups cooked rice

1 Place chicken in gallon-size plastic zipper bag. Add olive oil, lemon juice, and garlic. Seal bag closed and squeeze it gently to coat chicken with marinade. Leave an hour or more, or overnight if possible, in fridge.

2 Grill or pan fry chicken, seasoning with salt and fresh cracked pepper.

3 Serve over rice made according to package directions, or over salad greens and tossed with Cucumber Feta Salad.

Nutrition Snapshot
Per serving: 423 calories, 17g fat, 2g saturated fat, 42g protein, 27g carbs, 2g fiber, 0g sugar, 113mg sodium

Cucumber Feta Salad

Prep Time 10 minutes
Serves 6

1 English cucumber, unpeeled and diced (English cucumbers are more firm and will keep better until the next day to use in a lunch box)
1 cup cherry or grape tomatoes, cut in half
½ to ⅔ cup feta block cheese, crumbled
¼ cup finely chopped fresh Italian parsley leaves
Lemon dressing (recipe on the right)

1 Combine veggies, cheese, and parsley; toss with Lemon Dressing.

Nutrition Snapshot
Per serving: 120 calories, 11g fat, 2g saturated fat, 3g protein, 4g carbs, 1g fiber, 1g sugar, 284mg sodium

Lemon Dressing

Served here with: Watermelon cubes and 2 grape tomatoes, with the tips sliced off at a diagonal and pressed together to form a heart and secured with a pick.

4 Tbsp extra virgin olive oil
3 Tbsp lemon juice
½ tsp dried oregano
½ tsp salt
½ tsp fresh cracked black pepper
1 small clove garlic, crushed, or 1 cube frozen Crushed Garlic

1   Whisk together dressing ingredients.

Did You Know?

Cheese can only properly be called feta if it's made in Greece from at least 70 percent sheep's milk topped off with goat's milk, thanks to a 2002 decision by the European Union.

Sweet and Smokin' Hot

My husband loves meat flavored with lots of hot sauce, and I like a sweet barbecue sauce on my meat. I combined our two favorite flavors for a perfect blend of smoky, sweet, and spicy. This simple recipe can be cooked all day in a slow cooker. I guarantee that when you come home at the end of the day, the smell will make your mouth water. I like to cook a large batch of this for dinner since it's so versatile, and then use the leftovers in lunches throughout the week. Not only does it go well in a wrap, but also on a bun, in taco shells, or on a taco salad. It keeps well in the fridge, and freezes well.

Smoky Chipotle Barbecued Beef

Prep Time 10 minutes
Cook Time 10 hours in a slow cooker (unattended)
Serves 4 with leftovers

3 lbs lean beef roast – such as rump, eye of round, top round, flank
½ cup Kansas City Style Barbecue Sauce
1 (8-oz) can chipotle peppers in adobo sauce (you only need 3 or 4 peppers – the rest can be frozen to use later)

1 Place beef in slow cooker and pour barbecue sauce over beef.

2 Cut open each pepper and scrape seeds out and discard. Dice peppers and spread them on top of beef.

3 Cover and cook on low for 10 hours.

Nutrition Snapshot
Per serving: 317 calories, 7g fat, 2g saturated fat, 48g protein, 11g carbs, 1g fiber, 9g sugar, 547mg sodium

To Serve: include small sealed containers of sour cream and hot sauce.
Other suggestions: serve on taco shells, tortillas, buns, or over rice for dinner then enjoy the leftovers for lunch! To make a wrap, use 1 cup of barbequed beef and add diced tomatoes, fresh spinach or Romaine leaves, and 1 slice Cheddar or Pepper jack cheese.

Served here with: Tapioca pudding and cubed fresh fruit.

Did You Know?

Lexington, North Carolina claims to be the barbecue capital of the world. Surprisingly, it's not located in the Smokey Mountains.

Pasta-tively Delicious

Pasta primavera is a delicious dish, but it's usually high in fat. I made my version much lower in fat and easier to make. It's whipped up in the blender and simmered briefly on the stove. I also added chicken to boost the protein. Since primavera means "spring" in Italian, I topped it off with some "spring daffodils" made of yellow and green zucchini.

"Kristie has been such an inspiration to me. She started by making bentos as a creative outlet but has turned it into a healthy lifestyle. I've adapted this notion of eating healthy foods with correct portions because of her simple techniques and recipes. She has provided the resources to begin my journey into clean eating with a bento box. I've never been so excited about making lunches."
- Alicia Twomey Winget, Kristie's daughter-in-law

Pasta Primavera

Vegetarian

Prep Time 30 minutes
Cook Time 10 minutes
Serves 4

1 (12-oz) pkg Spinach Chive Linguine, about 3 cups cooked pasta
1 ½ cups 2% low fat cottage cheese
2 Tbsp cornstarch
1 (12-oz) can evaporated skim milk
1 clove garlic, crushed, or 1 cube frozen Crushed Garlic
2 tsp olive oil
2 tsp butter
½ tsp salt
¼ tsp cracked black pepper
1 egg
$^2/_3$ cup grated Parmesan and Romano cheese
1 tsp Dijon mustard
¼ cup frozen broccoli
¼ cup frozen asparagus spears
¼ cup frozen peas
¼ cup sliced carrot
¼ cup diced red bell pepper
1 small yellow and 1 small green zucchini squash

1 In blender, blend cottage cheese, cornstarch, and evaporated milk. Meanwhile, in a saucepan over medium heat, sauté garlic in olive oil. Stir in butter, salt and pepper, egg, Parmesan cheese, Dijon mustard, and the mixture from the blender. Heat until thickened, but don't bring to a full boil.

2 Combine broccoli, asparagus, peas, carrot, and bell pepper, and microwave until tender. In a large bowl, toss pasta, vegetables, and cooked sauce until well combined.

3 Peel yellow and green zucchini. Steam in microwave until softened. Cut zucchini horizontally into ¼ in pieces. Lay pieces flat on cutting board. Using two sizes of mini flower-shaped vegetable cutters, cut zucchini into "daffodil flowers".

4 Pour 1 ½ to 2 cups pasta mixture in the large compartment. Arrange zucchini daffodils on top.

Nutrition Snapshot
Per serving: 399 calories, 13g fat, 6g saturated fat, 29g protein, 41g carbs, 3g fiber, 17g sugar, 1,077mg sodium

Note: When eating it for lunch, toss the pasta and veggies with cooked chicken.

Served here with: Kiwi cut with a flower cutter, diced cooked chicken breast, and Parmesan cheese.

Did You Know?

Primavera gets its name from the Italian word for "spring" because the dish is like a colorful spring day. Like spaghetti with meatballs, pasta primavera is actually an Italian-American dish, popularized here in the United States.

Pack it For Work!

"The country is making a big mistake not teaching kids to cook and raise a garden and build fires."
— Loretta Lynn

Nina Holstead

I grew up in Germany, near the French border. My parents both love to cook and entertain, and I still cherish the weekends we spent driving to France, picking up wine at vineyards and shopping in French grocery stores. My mother always put a big emphasis on healthy eating. Early on, she taught us the benefits of organic and whole grain foods. She also taught me how to cook fast, healthy meals. From my father I learned to prepare the traditional German meals he made for us on Sundays. I still use many of the recipes they taught me. Cooking with my parents made me who I am. Both my parents taught me so much about food, wine, and family; I want to be able to teach my children with the same love.

I live in Connecticut with my husband and four children. I love cooking and baking, creating recipes and special dishes. I teach my kids to taste food and really pay attention. I want them to experience each unique spice, herb, fresh vegetable, and fruit so they know the flavor of unprocessed, natural food. My kids love trying my new creations and I have started to teach them how to make simple dishes. I want my boys to go to college knowing how to cook easy but healthy dishes and take that knowledge with them into their lives. For now, my kids are still young, and I get to enjoy cooking for them a little while longer. I love making them healthy bento-style lunches for school, and they love bringing them. I blog about these lunches at Mamabelly's Lunches With Love (mamabelly-luncheswithlove.blogspot.com). Food is my passion, and I hope to pass the gift of preparing and savoring it on to my children.

It's a Wrap!

I originally came up with this recipe to accommodate my husband's high-protein, unprocessed food diet. We pack six lunches every day, and I used to send his off with only the meat and wrap. I've gradually added ingredients to make it simple and inexpensive yet gourmet. Everyone from my 3-year-old to her dad loves this wrap!

I made this version one day when I was trying some different wrap options, and suddenly everyone was in the kitchen asking for a taste. Since this sandwich contains mostly chicken and guacamole, you need a lot of chicken to fill one deli-sized wrap. You can also make this with less meat by adding more lettuce, tomato, cucumber, carrot, celery, and perhaps a little cheese.

Guacamole Chicken Wrap

Prep Time 5 minutes
Cook Time 10 minutes
Serves 2

½ lb ground chicken
1 Tbsp vegetable oil
⅛ tsp salt
¼ tsp black pepper
1 (12-inch) Deli Wrap (or use 2 smaller whole-wheat tortillas, yielding two wraps)
3 Tbsp Avocado's Number Guacamole
1 cup torn butter lettuce leaves

1 Heat oil in a frying pan and add chicken. Cook thoroughly until not pink anymore. Season with salt and pepper and set aside to cool.

2 Spread guacamole on tortilla and add lettuce to cover, and then layer with cooled chicken.

3 Fold bottom of tortilla up and roll into a wrap, slice in half.

Nutrition Snapshot
Per serving: 218 calories, 13g fat, 3g saturated fat, 14g protein, 12g carbs, 3g fiber, 0g sugar, 223mg sodium

Served here with: Blue Corn Tortilla Chips, salsa, and cherry tomatoes.

Did You Know?

Guacamole was invented by Aztec Indians in Mexico. It became known as a Mexican dish after the Aztecs were conquered by the Spanish. "Mole" is the Spanish word for sauce, and "Guaca" is a Spanish translation of the Aztec word for avocado.

Pack it Veggie!

Vegetarian meals

"Do not eat garlic or onions; for their smell will reveal that you are a peasant."

— Cervantes, Don Quixote

Hmm. Well, I guess most of us are peasants then, since many delicious dishes rely heavily on these fragrant vegetables for their flavor. Go ahead: Proclaim your peasant status proudly!

"Going meatless once a week may reduce your risk of chronic preventable conditions like cancer, cardiovascular disease, diabetes and obesity. It can also help reduce your carbon footprint and save precious resources like fresh water and fossil fuel."

— meatlessmondays.com

Here is a collection of veggie-based dishes, rich in flavor, and perfect for Meatless Mondays.

You'll find additional vegetarian meals (or substitution ideas) throughout the book notated with this icon:

Vegetarian

Jenny Lester

Although I miss the daily activity of Lesterworld, one can never truly leave its influence. I'm a Junior Musical Theatre BFA student at Point Park University's Conservatory of Performing Arts in Pittsburgh, Pennsylvania. It's funny that it took my going away to school on the East Coast to realize I'm a Southern California girl, through and through. (Although everyone at school asks me why I'm so pale if I'm from L.A...oops) Being part of a rigorous conservatory program for the last two years has been revelatory and rewarding, as well as the most emotionally, physically, and mentally draining experience of my life.

Because of my insane schedule at school, I have learned to make my health a top priority. I don't have the luxury of showing up to a class exhausted and hungry; I have to be totally on my game, health-wise, to get the most out of my performance-based classes. Going to college far from home has been the perfect opportunity to take charge of my health and re-vamp my eating habits and the way I think about food.

During my freshman year of high school, my friend Brooke and I made an impulsive decision to become vegetarians. While I maintained the diet throughout high school, I never stopped to research what to eat. I now realize that just renouncing meat doesn't equal a healthy diet. It's been a long process, figuring out what works best for me when it comes to choosing foods, finding times to cook, and, of course, solidifying my lunch-packing routine. Recently, I've begun the transition toward eating mostly vegan, but I wanted to share a few of my all-time favorite vegetarian creations with you. I'm so proud of my mom for putting this book together, and I'm equally proud that she trusts me enough to have given me my own little corner. (Thanks, Mom!) Blogging between meals at: JennyLuisaLester.com

Greek Life, Greek Lunch

I start my day at 8 a.m. with ballet class, and I usually don't get home until well after 7 p.m. Some days we have only ten-minute breaks between rehearsals and classes and more rehearsals. On days like these, it's more sensible to pack small, healthy snacks rather than full meals I wouldn't have time to enjoy. I love this lunch because I can throw it together with no stress and nom* on it all day long!

Burger and Tabouli

Vegetarian

Prep Time 5 minutes
Cook Time 5 minutes
Serves 1

1 frozen **Vegetable Masala Burger**
4 oz pre-made **Tabouli** (about half the 7 oz container)
¼ cup **Greek olives**

1 Thaw burger and cut into bite-size pieces before adding it to the large compartment. Include Greek olives and prepared tabouli.

Nutrition Snapshot

Per serving: 235 calories, 16g fat, 2g saturated fat, 4g protein, 21g carbs, 2g fiber, 2g sugar, 590mg sodium

Served here with: Plain Greek yogurt and Ginger, Almond and Cashew Granola. Add granola to the Greek yogurt just before eating so that it doesn't get soggy.

*My mom asked me to define "nom." Somehow the Tumblr generation has taken this cartoonesque onomatopoeia for the sound of someone eating and turned it into a part of speech used to reference anything delicious.
Verb: "I want to nom that delicious food!"
Adjective: "That food looks so nomable."
Exclamation: Sees delicious food. "OMG, NOM!"

Kelly's Tip!

Live longer and healthier by eating yogurt. My parents have eaten yogurt since the 1950s and they are both healthy octogenarians. (I'm not saying there's a definite connection- -I'm just sayin'...) Studies show that yogurt containing live bacterial cultures may help you to live longer and may fortify your immune system. My favorite meal (yes, I have simple tastes) is a bowl of plain Greek yogurt with sliced banana and a little cereal or some crushed nuts. I eat it almost every day for either breakfast or lunch.

Wrap It Up and Go! (Go! Go!!)

School can get very overwhelming, and quickly. One minute I'll feel on top of the world, and the next minute I'll have a to-do list that would make the Energizer bunny cringe.

It's fabulous to have this simple, protein-packed lunch ready to grab and go (go. go. go. go). These wraps keep well, so I like to prepare them on Sunday night, and then pack them for lunch or dinner throughout the week.

Work It Out Veggie Wraps

Vegetarian

Prep Time 5 minutes
Serves 4

4 large whole wheat tortillas
4 Tbsp Red Pepper Spread with Eggplant and Garlic
4 Tbsp cream cheese or Neufchâtel cheese
8 Tbsp canned black beans, drained
2 Persian cucumbers, sliced lengthwise
1 (6-oz) bag fresh baby spinach
1 avocado, thinly sliced

1   Spread Red Pepper Spread liberally on one half of each tortilla—make sure it doesn't get too close to the edges! Spread cream cheese on the other half of each tortilla. Spoon black beans down center of each tortilla.

2   To each tortilla, add a few cucumber strips, a small bunch of spinach, and some avocado slices. Don't add too much of anything or you'll have trouble keeping the wraps closed.

3   Fold each tortilla in on both ends and roll wrap tightly. Cut wrap in half.

Nutrition Snapshot

Per serving: 276 calories, 12g fat, 3g saturated fat, 10g protein, 32g carbs, 7g fiber, 1g sugar, 374mg sodium

Note: To make this vegan, substitute the cream cheese with Non-Dairy Cream Cheese spread.

Served here with: Hard-boiled egg, cut veggies with dip, and trail mix.

 **Kelly's Tip!**

You can secure a wrap by inserting a long food pick through it. If the food pick is topped with a decorative accent, even better! My favorite source for these and other bento supplies is www.BentoUSA.com.

Did You Know?

Neufchâtel cheese is cream cheese that's lower in fat than regular cream cheese because it's made from a combination of cream and whole milk. Authentic Neufchâtel is from France and doesn't contain any cream at all.

Desperately Seeking Sustenance

This fun (and super easy) meal was created by accident. Our university is located in downtown Pittsburgh, so it's inconvenient and expensive to keep a car at school. Since the nearest Trader Joe's is a 30-minute bus ride away, we shop for groceries only once every two to three weeks. (It's seriously a religious pilgrimage!) During those last few days before our next trip, as we're all running out of food, necessity becomes the mother of invention. One such weekend, my friends and I got together to create some semblance of a dinner from whatever food we had left. Thus, the Mandatory Meatless Meatball Scramble was born, and there was even extra for lunch the next day.

Mandatory Meatless Meatball Scramble

Vegetarian

Prep Time 5 minutes
Cook Time 5 minutes
Serves 3

4 eggs
2 cups frozen pre-cooked Organic Brown Rice, thawed
¼ cup marinara sauce
6-8 frozen Meatless Meatballs
½ bag baby spinach (3 oz)

1   Place brown rice in a medium saucepan. Break eggs into pan and begin scrambling them in with the rice.

2   Meanwhile, pour marinara sauce over meatballs in a microwave-safe dish and heat in microwave for 2 minutes. Mash meatballs with fork and return to microwave until heated through.

3   Continue scrambling rice and eggs. Add baby spinach to rice mixture. Add cooked and mashed meatballs into rice mixture. Remove from heat and stir mixture. Let cool.

Nutrition Snapshot

Per serving: 163 calories, 3g fat, 0g saturated fat, 8g protein, 27g carbs, 3g fiber, 0g sugar, 279mg sodium

Served here with: Pre-packaged Pineapple Spears and cottage cheese.

Did You Know?

"Meatless" meat can be made out of soy (think tofu and tempeh), or the protein part of wheat gluten (seitan pronounced "say-tan"). Many vegetarians actually avoid seitan as they think the texture is too "meaty."

Jazzersalad

During the warmer months of the year, the university dance studios can get very hot. Most days we walk around school wearing a half dance-clothes/half pajamas ensemble, water bottle in hand. After a particularly hot and grueling morning, I have no appetite for a heavy lunch. This cold salad is the perfect light meal, yet it's filling enough to keep me from getting hungry during the second half of my day.

Lentil and Quinoa Salad

*Vegetarian
Gluten Free*

Prep Time 5 Minutes
Cook Time 15-20 Minutes
Serves 4

1 cup uncooked Organic Tri-Color Quinoa
1 (14.75-oz) jar marinated artichoke hearts, drained
½ cup Greek Olives
1 cucumber
1 large tomato
1 avocado
1 (4-oz) container Mediterranean Crumbled Feta
1 (17.6-oz) pkg refrigerated Steamed Lentils
2 Tbsp Goddess Dressing

1 Cook quinoa according to package directions. Set aside to cool.

2 Cut artichoke hearts, olives, cucumber, tomato, and avocado into small pieces.

3 Combine quinoa and vegetables with the remaining ingredients and enjoy! (Pack the dressing separately if you won't be eating this within a few hours.)

Nutrition Snapshot

Per serving: 576 calories, 23g fat, 5g saturated fat, 26g protein, 68g carbs, 18g fiber, 7g sugar, 1,004mg sodium

Note: To make it vegan, use soy cheese in place of the crumbled feta.

Served here with: Sliced banana and Almond Butter with Flaxseeds—
Mix in raisins and chocolate chips and eat with banana!

Pack it Veggie!

"The doctor of the future will no longer treat the human frame with drugs, but rather will cure and prevent disease with nutrition." — Thomas Edison

Nimali Fernando

I am a pediatrician and the mother of two young boys. Consequently, I am very aware of the increasing rates of childhood obesity and diet-related illness. At home, I work hard to expose my children to a world of whole foods, gardening, farmers markets, and healthy meals cooked in our kitchen. At work, I have made it my passion to help my patients and their families understand the importance of good nutrition. I strive to be an example of a working mother who finds the time to prepare good food.

In 2011 I started my website, Doctor Yum (DoctorYum.com), to show parents how to prepare healthy, fast recipes for families with kids of all ages. I provide advice about how to raise kids who make healthy food choices in a world of junk food. All recipes on my site are tasted by the Tiny Tasters, a panel of kids in my community. We also post videos of the Tiny Tasters trying new foods. I try to show that kids can be taught to love healthy food if it is presented with love, patience, and a positive attitude.

In 2012 I am launching a non-profit, called The Doctor Yum Project, a hands-on effort to teach kids the joys and benefits of healthy eating. My partners and I will be working with students in a school garden; providing cooking and grocery shopping classes in lower income neighborhoods; and expanding a program that helps local restaurants improve their kids' menu options. I also serve on the Committee on Obesity for the Virginia Chapter of the American Academy of Pediatrics. I'm working to show other medical providers how a few moments of dietary counseling can make a dramatic difference in the health of a child.

"Doctor Yum has taught our family the importance of persistence, particularly when it comes to vegetables. We regularly offer new foods to try and then keep offering them, even if the dish wasn't well received. Many times that same dish has become a hit after seeing it again and trying it again. It's really become a lot of fun seeing how the children's palates, diet, and even attitude have changed. Thanks Doctor Yum!"
- Kara, mom to five of Doctor Yum's patients

213

Asian Elation Very Veggie Lunch

Last year my 9-year-old asked that we cook more vegetarian meals together. As I know the health benefits of a plant-based diet, I readily agreed. This meal can be eaten hot for dinner, and there will be enough left over for a cold lunch. I rely on these kinds of time-saving, double-duty recipes. The tempeh is a great protein for vegetarian dishes. It quickly takes on the flavors of sauces and has a great texture. My Tiny Tasters have come to like tempeh for these reasons. The quinoa, though not a usual Asian ingredient, also absorbs the Asian flavors.

Asian Veggies and Tempeh Over Quinoa

Vegetarian

Prep Time 15 minutes
Cook time 20 minutes
Serves 4

1 cup uncooked quinoa (red or brown can be used)
4 Tbsp soy sauce
1 Tbsp sesame oil
1 Tbsp rice wine vinegar
1 tsp grated ginger
2 cloves garlic, minced, or 2 cubes frozen Crushed Garlic
1 Tbsp honey
1 (8-oz) pkg 3 Grain Tempeh, plain, cut into ½-inch cubes
1 Tbsp vegetable oil
1 cup broccoli, cut in small pieces
2 carrots, peeled and chopped
2 cups chopped baby bok choy (green and white parts)

1 Cook quinoa according to package directions.

2 Whisk soy sauce, sesame oil, vinegar, ginger, garlic, and honey in a medium-sized bowl. Add tempeh and stir to coat. Marinate tempeh for about 10-15 minutes while prepping veggies.

3 Heat vegetable oil in a large stir-fry pan. Remove tempeh with a slotted spoon and stir-fry until slightly browned, about 3-4 minutes. Add veggies and about half of the tempeh marinade. Continue to cook veggies for additional 3-4 minutes. Combine cooked quinoa with remaining marinade, stirring to incorporate all the marinade and vegetables into quinoa. Serve hot or cold.

Nutrition Snapshot
Per serving: 413 calories, 16g fat, 2g saturated fat, 17g protein, 49g carbs, 9g fiber, 8g sugar, 560mg sodium

Served here with: Edamame and Freeze Dried Mango.

Did You Know?

Tempeh (which originated in Indonesia) and tofu (which originated in China) are both made from soybeans. Tempeh incorporates the whole bean, so it has more fiber, vitamins, and protein than tofu.

I Can't Believe It's Not Chicken!

Last summer I had an amazing mock-chicken-salad wrap at a great vegetarian grocery store in Hawaii. After tasting this creation, I was determined to create my own. Chicken salad can be quite heavy when prepared with lots of mayonnaise. In my version the creaminess comes from yogurt, while mustard and honey give it a sweet tanginess. This salad can be served on naan bread, a whole-wheat wrap, or mini baguettes from Trader Joe's.

Chicken-less Salad

Prep Time 10 minutes
Serves 3

⅓ **cup plain low fat yogurt**
1 tsp Dijon mustard
1 tsp honey
1 (8-oz) pkg Chicken-less Strips, cut into ½-inch cubes
¼ **cup grapes, quartered**
2 Tbsp diced red onion
2 Tbsp chopped walnuts
1 Tbsp chopped chives
Salt to taste
Black pepper to taste

1 In a medium bowl, whisk together yogurt, mustard, and honey.

2 Toss chicken-less strips, grapes, red onions, walnuts, and chives in dressing until well-coated. Season with salt and pepper to taste.

3 Serve with naan bread, in a whole wheat tortilla wrap or on Trader Joe's mini baguettes.

Nutrition Snapshot
Per serving: 174 calories, 5g fat, 1g saturated fat, 22g protein, 9g carbs, 2g fiber, 5g sugar, 384mg sodium

Bountiful Blueberry Jello

Fruit jello is a great way to get kids to eat fresh fruit. It can be made with any pure juice with real fruit stirred in. I use blueberry juice with real blueberries for a burst of bountiful antioxidants. This vegetarian version of jello uses agar-agar as the thickening agent instead of gelatin, which is usually made from animal products. Agar-agar, which is made from seaweed, comes in flake or powder form and can be found in many health-food stores or Asian markets.

Prep Time 5 min
Refrigerate 2-3 hours or overnight
Serves 4

1 qt Trader Joe's Blueberry Juice
4-5 Tbsp agar-agar flakes (or 4 tsp powder)
1 pinch sea salt
¾ **cup frozen or fresh blueberries**
2 Tbsp honey or agave

1 Place juice, agar-agar, salt, and honey into medium saucepan over high heat, stirring to dissolve the flakes. Bring to a boil, reduce flame and simmer for 3-4 minutes, stirring occasionally. (When you can see that the agar-agar is fully dissolved, it's done.)

2 Place a small handful of blueberries in the medium compartment of your EasyLunchbox container and pour the hot liquid over it. Remaining jello and blueberries can be set up in additional lunch containers or other serving dishes.

3 Chill until jelled.

Nutrition Snapshot
Per serving: 75 calories, 0g fat, 0g saturated fat, 2g protein, 16g carbs, 10g fiber, 3g sugar, 12mg sodium

Served here with: Sugar snap peas and baby carrots.

Pack it Vegan!

Vegan meals

"*Scientific studies supported by the American Dietetic Association confirm that vegan and vegetarian diets are associated with lower cholesterol, lower risk of heart disease, lower blood pressure, lower risk of hypertension and Type 2 diabetes, lower body fat, and lower overall cancer rates. ...a vegan diet can actually reverse diabetes, heart disease, and even cancer.*" – Going VEGAN with ellen (vegan.ellen.warnerbros.com)

You'll find additional vegan meals (or substitution ideas) throughout the book notated with this icon:

Alina Joy Dubois

When I was in college, my roommate and I challenged ourselves to become vegans. This wasn't a huge switch for me because I had grown up in a vegetarian home. Still, I was giving up some much-loved treats for the sake of better health. Excited, we purchased our first all-vegan cookbook. The food was delicious, but the recipes took forever to prepare! Turning to the back of the book, we discovered why: Our cookbook had been written by a monk. He was not just an ordinary monk, but a monk who was in charge of the kitchen. In other words, he had a lot of time to devote to meal preparation. As students, we didn't have that luxury. That book sat unused on our bookshelf for the rest of the year.

Fast forward 15 years. I'm still vegan, but now I'm also a wife and mother of three young children living on our small family farm in North Texas. (If you feel like you're in the minority eating vegan, try doing it on a five-acre fruit orchard in the middle of cattle country!) I still don't have hours to spend in the kitchen, but I do want to provide my family with the best, most nourishing food possible. For a recipe to be a hit in my kitchen, it needs to taste great, be simple and quick to make, and use ingredients I'm likely to have on hand.

Eating fresh, easy-to-prepare meals goes hand in hand with farming. In 2010, my husband left his career as a software engineer and took up farming to spend more time with our children. We call our farm "The Good Old Days Farm" to remind us that we'll look back on this time and say, "Those were the good old days!" If you come by for a visit, you'll get some good, old-fashioned home cooking. We'll walk you through our orchards and gardens, tell you farm stories, and introduce you to our alpacas, Carob and Mr. Vanilla. You can even meet the family duck. If you can't stop by in person, visit us online at the Good Old Days Farm (GoodOldDaysFarm.com). I also coordinate Outdoor Schoolhouse (OutdoorSchoolhouse.com), a blog where several talented writers come together to share stories and lessons about what we can learn from nature. I hope to see you there!

Guyana Finish That Rice?

This is a recipe I learned when I lived in Guyana from 1999 to 2000. We had limited access to electricity, so the ongoing local joke was, "Every day here is Y2K!" We could not rely on refrigeration, so all our meals had to be made fresh each day. My friends "Big John" and Ruth owned a grocery stall in Staerbrook Market, the main market in Guyana's capital city of Georgetown. Sometimes, I would go to the market and help them. Ruth would make CookUp Rice at home in the morning, and we would eat it for lunch. By then it was no longer hot, but it was still delicious.

Another time I was at a wedding and was surprised to see hot CookUp Rice as the main dish of the wedding feast. First, they handed each person a warm calabash leaf to use as a plate. Next, they scooped CookUp Rice onto the middle of the leaf and added seven types of curried vegetable dishes around the edge of the rice. I think this was the best wedding food I have ever tasted, partly because the food was delicious, and partly because we ate with our fingers instead of forks. (To think that my mother spent the entire summer before I moved to South America reminding me about my table manners. She said that I had to have exemplary etiquette or the people in Guyana would think all North Americans "eat that way." So I was sure to ask someone to take a picture of us eating with our fingers and enjoying every bite!)

CookUp Rice

Vegan
Gluten Free

Prep Time 15 minutes
Cook Time 45 minutes
Serves 4

2 cups long grain brown rice
1 (14-oz) can light or regular coconut milk *
4 cups water
2 cloves garlic, finely chopped, or 2 cubes frozen Crushed Garlic,
1 small onion, chopped
1 carrot, grated
1 ½ cups cooked black-eyed peas
Salt to taste

1 Combine all ingredients in a large pot and bring mixture to a boil.

2 Reduce heat to simmer and continue cooking until all liquid has been absorbed and rice is soft enough to eat. Add salt to taste and enjoy!

Nutrition Snapshot
Per serving: 273 calories, 6g fat, 4g saturated fat, 6g protein, 49g carbs, 7g fiber, 1g sugar, 318mg sodium

* TJ's only carries light coconut milk and it works fine, but for authentic version, use full-fat coconut milk

Served here with: Kale and cherry tomato salad (with a twist of lemon and olive oil) and Freeze Dried Banana Chips and Low Salt Peanuts.

Did You Know?

Guyana is the only country in mainland South America where English is the official language. This makes it very easy to order CookUp Rice when you're there, although it's easy enough to simply make it yourself!

Little Lettuce Boat Lunch

I first discovered lettuce boats when they were served to me at a bridal shower. They are so easy to make and eat that they quickly became a favorite around our house. These are great at home, in lunch boxes, on picnics, and just about everywhere else. For long road trips, I close them up with a bento pick and pack them in my EasyLunchbox containers. It's a no-fuss way to travel that helps us eat vegetables and avoid fast food. The sprouts give the lettuce boats such a nice crunchy texture that your family will never guess something this delicious is so good for them. I won't tell them if you don't!

Lettuce Boats

Prep Time 10 minutes
Cook Time None
Serves 6

1 pkg endive, baby romaine lettuce leaves, or curly red leaf lettuce
1 (19-oz) pkg soft tofu
3 medium avocados
2 cloves garlic, finely chopped, or 2 cubes frozen Crushed Garlic, thawed
Juice of 1 lemon
1 small onion, finely chopped
2 tomatoes, finely diced
½ tsp salt
½ cup pine nuts (optional)
4 cups alfalfa, broccoli, clover, and/or radish sprouts

1   Wash and separate lettuce leaves. Set aside to dry.

2   In a bowl, smash together tofu and avocados. Add garlic, lemon juice, onion, tomatoes, salt, and pine nuts. Stir together.

3   Taking a lettuce leaf in your hand, scoop about ¼ cup tofu-avocado mixture into the leaf and spread. Place a layer of about ½ cup sprouts over avocado mixture. Garnish with more diced tomatoes and pine nuts if desired. Fold edges of lettuce over each other and fasten in place with a cute bento pick.

Note: Choose your lettuce based on how "sturdy" you want your boat to be!

Nutrition Snapshot
Per serving: 303 calories, 24g fat, 2g saturated fat, 12g protein, 14g carbs, 8g fiber, 1g sugar, 230mg sodium

Served here with: Lentil salad (with cherry tomatoes, chopped kale, lemon juice and olive oil) and watermelon chunks.

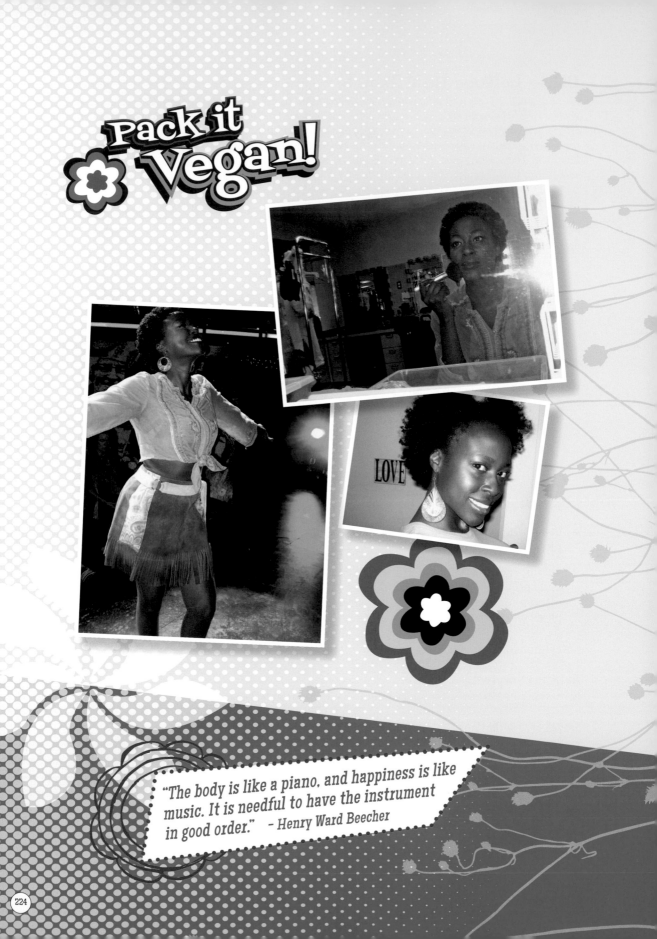

Pack it Vegan!

"The body is like a piano, and happiness is like music. It is needful to have the instrument in good order." – Henry Ward Beecher

Christine Horn

I've been a vegan for a little over a year now. This makes me laugh because I was the last person on earth I thought would become vegan. I have Bermudian and Jamaican roots, so I grew up eating curry chicken, goat, oxtails, and more. I decided to be vegan to live a healthier lifestyle, and because I began to care more about animals.

Eating a plant-based diet is not a challenge, and I still cook with the same flair I've always had. My love of cooking began with my mother, who taught me how to cook starting when I was eight. These days, I substitute veggies for the meat she used. I really enjoy eating everything nature has to offer.

Inadvertently, I've become somewhat of a health advocate. I love sharing healthy eating tips with friends and family. I was moved to start a blog, Wings to Weeds (wingstoweeds.com), and a cooking show to share my love of vegetables with the world.

"Before I met Christine I was turned off by vegan food because my previous experiences were tasteless and nasty. Once Christine started cooking for me I began to love vegan food. I never feel like anything is missing from my meals when she cooks. I still love chicken and fish, but these days I ask her for the veggies instead." - Wendel Henry, Christine's boyfriend of 4 years

Christine Horn is an American actress of the stage and screen who splits her time between Los Angeles and Atlanta. She has appeared in a lengthy list of regional theatrical productions, feature films, and the Broadway, Las Vegas, and national tour companies of Disney's The Lion King. Christine is also a noted singer/ songwriter who has released two CDs on iTunes and is currently working on a new project. When she is not acting, Christine is hosting Wings to Weeds, a vegan cooking show she created and produced. She believes in creating her own opportunities.

Slap Yo Mama Burger

Even though I don't eat meat, every now and then I crave a burger. When I want something filled with flavor and spice, I make this one. The first time I made it, I really did want to slap somebody because it was that good! You can trade the burger out for whatever you like, but I think you'll love this one.

Full of Spice Vegan Burger (Vegan)

Prep Time 5 minutes
Cook Time 12 minutes
Makes 4 sandwiches

1 (10-oz) box frozen Vegetable Masala Burgers (4 burgers)
1 Tbsp extra virgin olive oil
1 cup sliced onions
Pinch sea salt
½ tsp black pepper
4 pieces Lavash Bread or Whole Wheat Bread
1 cup fresh spinach
1 sliced tomatoes
1 cup clover or alfalfa sprouts
½ cup Salsa Especial or Mild Salsa

1 Over medium heat, sauté burgers for 10-15 minutes or until cooked through. Flip burgers after 5 minutes so cooking will be even.

2 Remove cooked burgers and set aside. To the same skillet, add oil, onions, salt, and pepper. Cook onions until they are soft and slightly brown. Remove from heat.

3 Lay lavash bread on a plate. Begin stacking ingredients starting with spinach, tomatoes, sprouts, burger, 2 tablespoons of salsa, and sautéed onions.

4 If using lavash bread, fold over the sides from right to left then fold the tops down. Wrap sandwich in foil to hold it together. Take a big bite and ENJOY!

Nutrition Snapshot
Per sandwich: 404 calories, 13g fat, 1g saturated fat, 11g protein, 63g carbs, 7g fiber, 4g sugar, 909mg sodium

Served here with: White Corn Tortilla Chips and salsa.

Did You Know?

"Masala" is a word from India that means "mixture of spices."

Ready, Set, Salad!

As an actor, while living and auditioning in Los Angeles, I spend a lot of time in the car and in traffic. It's important for me to think ahead and to keep snacks and meals in my lunch bag. When I have only a few minutes before I have to run out the door for an audition, I can make this refreshing and filling salad quickly. I chose this recipe to share with you because a lot of people are used to the traditional romaine or iceberg lettuce salads. My five-minute meal goes against the grain.

Ensalada Verde (Green Salad)

Prep Time 5 minutes
Cook Time 3 minutes
Serves 2

Vegan
Gluten Free

1 (10-oz) bag sliced crimini mushrooms
2 Tbsp extra virgin olive oil
¼ tsp garlic salt
¼ tsp black pepper
4 cups freshly washed spinach
1 (12-oz) container pico de gallo
4 Tbsp Tuscan Italian Dressing with Balsamic Vinegar, or your favorite dressing

1 Heat olive oil in skillet. Add crimini mushrooms and sauté until golden brown and tender. Season with garlic salt and pepper.

2 Remove mushrooms from skillet once cooked and on a paper towel lined plate to remove excess oil.

3 In a large bowl, combine spinach and pico de gallo. Toss with your favorite salad dressing. Add mushrooms to mixed salad and serve.

Nutrition Snapshot

Per serving: 238 calories, 17g fat, 2g saturated fat, 7g protein, 22g carbs, 3g fiber, 10g sugar, 831mg sodium

Served here with: Cucumber slices and raw almonds.

Did You Know?

The term "salad days" comes from Shakespeare. (What doesn't?) It's a line spoken by Cleopatra, describing her younger self as "green in judgment" and "cold."
(You know, like a lettuce leaf.)

Pack it Vegan!

Leslie teaches Tristin and Tyler to make vegan "Earthburger" sliders at Harlem's City Cookhouse.

Leslie Durso

I was first bitten by the food bug when I was seven, watching my grandmother and great-grandmother hold court in their Italian kitchen as they whipped up Sunday dinners. Lucky for me, they indulged my curiosity. They gave me step-by-step instructions and a treasure trove of family recipes that migrated from Naples, Italy to Little Italy, New York, to my home in Los Angeles. These memories and the influence of Southern California have shaped my food philosophy. At the ripe age of eight, I declared myself a vegetarian, an unpopular position in a household of six meat-eaters. By then I was already preparing the bulk of the family dinners. When Food Network launched in 1993, this 13-year-old was glued to cooking shows. While my girlfriends were dishing Beverly Hills 90210, I was cooking with Lidia Bastianich.

While majoring in English at University of Colorado, I was wooed to Los Angeles and New York City for a modeling career, which quickly led to an acting career. From theater to comedies to soap operas, I kept busy. It wasn't until an educational hosting stint on Discovery Channel with Bill Nye the Science Guy that I discovered my aha moment.

Today I share my passion for whole food on LeslieDurso.com, and in live appearances on TV and throughout the web — Food Network, Discovery Channel, Mother Nature Network — with my kinder gentler, meat-free message. I hope to inspire life-long healthy eating habits by bridging the gap between the meaties and the meatless. To quote Maxim Magazine: "We want to hire Leslie as our own personal chef! We'll even eat vegetables for her." Yay! I hope my continued engagement online and in the media will spread the wellness benefits of plant-based eating to a broader swath of eaters, including mainstream omnivores, my fellow millennials, and especially kids. I lend my support to a number of animal rights charities including The Humane Society, Best Friends Animal Rescue, People for the Ethical Treatment of Animals (PETA), and Farm Sanctuary through promotional support and appearances.

Stuffed Sunday Lunch

My grandmother's stuffed peppers were always a favorite at the Sunday dinner table. She used beef, but no one will even notice that my hearty and delicious recipe is meat-less. Don't tell my Nona! Kick up the heat a notch on cold days by sprinkling some cayenne into the filling while simmering.

Italian Stuffed Peppers

Prep time 15 minutes
Cook Time 10 minutes
Serves 4

4 red bell peppers
1 medium onion, diced
4 cloves garlic, chopped, or 4 cubes frozen Crushed Garlic
3 Tbsp olive oil
1 (12-oz) pkg Beef-less Ground Beef
1 (10.5-oz) pkg fully cooked brown rice
1 (18-oz) jar Traditional Marinara Sauce
1 tsp dried basil
½ tsp dried oregano
⅓ cup pine nuts, toasted

1 Preheat oven using broil setting. Slice bell peppers lengthwise and scoop out seeds and ribs. Place peppers cut side up on a baking sheet and broil for 3-5 minutes or until peppers are slightly soft but still firm. Remove from oven and set aside.

2 In a large frying pan over medium heat, sauté onions and garlic in olive oil for 3-4 minutes or until onions are soft. Add beef-less beef and brown rice, stirring and breaking it up with a spoon. Sauté for 2 minutes and add marinara sauce, basil, oregano, and pine nuts. Sauté for a few minutes to warm through.

3 Stuff pepper halves with rice mixture. Serve at room temp or heat in a microwave.

Nutrition Snapshot
Per serving: 499 calories, 21g fat, 2g saturated fat, 22g protein, 59g carbs, 11g fiber, 5g sugar, 1,211mg sodium

Balsamic Glazed Strawberries

6 large ripe strawberries
2 Tbsp balsamic vinegar
2 Tbsp brown sugar

1 Place the vinegar and sugar in a saucepan on medium heat. Stir until the sugar is dissolved and simmering. Remove from heat and set aside.

2 Rinse and dry the strawberries. Pour the glaze over the strawberries and toss to coat.

Nutrition Snapshot
Per serving: 21 calories, 0g fat, 0g saturated fat, 0g protein, 6g carbs, 1g fiber, 5g sugar, 4mg sodium

Served here with: Greek Olive Medley.

Did You Know?

Balsamic vinegar is made from white grape juice while red wine
vinegar is made from grape juice that has actually fermented into wine.

Take a Hike Power-Packed Lunch

Living in SoCal means lots of impromptu hikes with friends and my rescue dog Pepé. If I were to pack a lunch for a long hike, this would be it. My Yummy Barley Salad is packed full of protein, fiber, vitamins, and flavor. The best part is that you can make this a day ahead of time and keep it in the fridge.

Yummy Barley Salad
Vegan

Prep Time 5 minutes
Cook Time 45 minutes
Serves 6

2 cups barley
4 cups vegetable broth
1 medium yellow onion, diced
4 cloves garlic, chopped, or 4 cubes frozen Crushed Garlic
1 (17.6-oz) pkg refrigerated Steamed Lentils
1 (8-oz) pkg refrigerated Steamed and Peeled Baby Beets, quartered
½ cup sliced almonds, toasted
½ tsp salt, divided
½ tsp black pepper
2 cups arugula

1 In a large pot, sauté onions and garlic with ¼ tsp salt for 5 minutes on medium until onions are soft. Pour in vegetable broth and bring to a boil. Add barley. Stir, cover, and reduce heat to a simmer. Cook for 30-40 minutes or until grains are tender. Fluff with a fork.

2 Add lentils, beets, almonds, remaining salt, and pepper. Let cool and stir in arugula.

Nutrition Snapshot
Per serving: 253 calories, 4g fat, 0g saturated fat, 12g protein, 42g carbs, 12g fiber, 8g sugar, 505mg sodium

Served here with: Simply the Best Trek Mix and Triple Fruit Treat.

Did You Know?

Malted barley is used to make beer, whisky, malt vinegar, and yes, malts.
Malting is a process in which barley is soaked in water until it sprouts.
The sprouted barley is dried in a kiln.

Asian Take-out from Home

Forget the greasy Chinese take-out. It always arrives late and cold anyway. Make these easy-to-prepare gyozas at home instead. They are delicious at any temperature and make a satisfying meal when accompanied by soy-sautéed veggies and healthy brown rice. Spare ribs and pork-fried are so yesterday!

Vegetable Gyoza over Brown Rice and Veggies

Prep Time 5 minutes
Cook Time 15 minutes
Serves 4

1 (16-oz) pkg frozen Vegetable Gyozas, prepared according to package directions
2 (11-oz) pkgs refrigerated Asparagus Sauté mix
1 Tbsp vegetable oil
2 (10-oz) pouches frozen fully cooked brown rice, prepared according to package directions
2 Tbsp sesame seeds, toasted
Asian Sauce (recipe below)

1 In a large pan over medium heat, sauté asparagus with vegetable oil for approximately 5 minutes, or until fork tender. Remove from heat.

2 Prepare Asian Sauce and add half the recipe to vegetables. Stir to coat.

3 Place ¼ of the brown rice in the large compartment. Add ¼ of the asparagus sauté veggies. Place ¼ of the gyozas on top and drizzle with the remaining sauce. Finish by sprinkling with toasted sesame seeds. This dish can be eaten at room temperature, but is ideal to be reheated in a microwave.

Asian Sauce

½ cup water
4 Tbsp rice wine vinegar
2 Tbsp agave nectar
2 Tbsp soy sauce
2 tsp cornstarch mixed with 2 Tbsp water

1 In a small pot, bring water, vinegar, agave, and soy sauce to a simmer. Add cornstarch mixture. Remove from heat and stir until thick.

Nutrition Snapshot

Per serving: 640 calories, 18g fat, 2g saturated fat, 15g protein, 107g carbs, 10g fiber, 21g sugar, 596mg sodium

Served here with: Prepared edamame and Thai Lime Chili Cashews.

Kelly's Tip!

"Gyoza" is the Japanese word for the dumplings known as potstickers. Don't let the name mislead you: if you use a non-stick pot, they won't have to live up to their name.

Pack it Gluten-Free!

Substitutions Made Yummy

If you're following a gluten-free diet by choice or by necessity, you're not alone. These days it's easier than ever to find gluten-free foods in stores and online. Living without gluten does not mean living without your favorite foods. There are ways to make almost every recipe gluten-free. The following pages contain eight delicious meals created by gals who avoid gluten, either for themselves or someone in their family.

You'll find other gluten-free recipes (or gluten-free substitution ideas for some) marked throughout the book, notated with this icon:

Gluten Free

Patrick and Julia with my Cowardly Lion bento

Lauri Fitzsimmons

I'm the mom of a 13-year-old boy who decided at an early age that dancing was his life. He's had some amazing opportunities: meeting renowned dancers like Mikhail Baryshnikov and Savion Glover, and studying with many of the celebrity dancers and choreographers from *So You Think You Can Dance.*

I love that my son is a performer. I come from five generations of performers and found my niche in improv comedy for years. Some of my best times on stage were riffing with my fellow actors, never knowing what craziness was going to ensue. And that's exactly what it's like being a parent to Patrick! Craziness abounds, and there are laughs and silliness everywhere. When I found joy in creating silly bento lunches for my son, I felt right in my element. I knew he could get a giggle in the middle of the day simply looking at his lunch. (Sometimes I even surprise my husband Doug with a goofy lunch to catch him off-guard.)

Patrick is constantly in dance class, or off to auditions or rehearsal, so we're on the road a lot. It's a lot of fun, but it puts me in a quandary: I suffer from severe gluten intolerance, so I have to be prepared on the road. That's where education and an easy packing plan come in handy.

Enter EasyLunchboxes, which made it a breeze to pack and take my meals with me. Then, in one of those once-in-a-lifetime occurrences where fates coincide, I came to know Kelly herself. One day I noticed a post she had written on her EasyLunchboxes blog about teaching at a youth theater camp the previous summer. I wrote to her, asking about the camp because I knew Patrick would enjoy it. Well! After several emails back and forth, not only did we discover that we had several friends in common, but our own children had just started rehearsal, together, in a production of *The Wizard of Oz!* Her daughter Julia was playing Dorothy, and Patrick was playing the Cowardly Lion. And that was how a very special friendship was born.

Keep Your Pinky Up!

One of the niceties I miss on a gluten-free diet is the English tradition of afternoon tea. All those lovely finger sandwiches and lifting one's pinky while sipping a cup of Earl Grey. Phooey! Now I can create my own tasty finger sandwiches with Trader Joe's gluten-free breads. Pip pip! Cheerio!

English Tea Sandwiches

Gluten Free
Vegetarian
Omit salmon

Prep Times 10 minutes
Cook Time 20 minutes (for hard boiled eggs)
Serves 4

4 slices gluten-free bread
6 eggs
1 ripe avocado, mashed
3 Tbsp mayonnaise
1 Tbsp yellow mustard
1 Tbsp pickle relish
1 Tbsp chopped onion
1 Tbsp chopped celery
1 (8-oz) pkg smoked salmon

1 Place eggs in medium saucepan and fill with water to cover eggs by 1 inch. Bring water to low boil then turn off heat. Let sit for 17 minutes, then drain and refill with ice water. Once cooled, peel eggs.

2 Chop hard-boiled eggs and add mayonnaise, mustard, relish, onion, and celery. Combine thoroughly.

3 Cut off bread crusts and cut in half lengthwise to provide 8 rectangular slices of bread. Top each slice of bread with a layer of mashed avocado, then a spoonful of egg salad mixture. On top of each sandwich, place a layer or two of sliced smoked salmon.

Nutrition Snapshot

Per serving: 420 calories, 22g fat, 4g saturated fat, 25g protein, 33g carbs, 5g fiber, 5g sugar, 1,163mg sodium

Served here with: Meringue Cookies and Dark Chocolate Covered Power Berries.

Did You Know?

The British used to have two "tea meals": afternoon tea and high tea. Afternoon tea was a snack of small sandwiches, finger food, and pastries served between midday lunch and a late evening supper. High tea was served after work, around 5 p.m., and included a hot dish or cold cuts. If you were in the upper class, you could conceivably have breakfast, luncheon, afternoon tea, high tea, and supper (and no doubt finish your day with an antacid).

Happy Tummy Meal

Living a gluten-free life, I do sometimes miss a good chicken nugget. I sure don't miss the fat, so I came up with a way to make my own baked version. They taste even better than what the fast food restaurants serve. Now all I need is the toy that comes with them.

A Good Chicken Nugget

 Gluten Free

Prep Time 15 minutes
Cook Time 15 minutes
Serves 4

1 (1.5-lb) pkg boneless skinless chicken breast, cut into bite-size pieces
2 Tbsp Sassy Seasoning Mix (recipe below)
1 cup all-purpose gluten-free flour
2 egg whites, beaten in shallow bowl

1   Preheat oven to 450° F.

2   Add 2 Tbsp of Sassy Seasoning mix to 1 cup gluten-free flour and combine thoroughly.

3   One at a time, place chicken pieces in the egg whites first, and then dredge them in flour mixture and place on non-stick baking sheet. Discard any remaining flour mixture, since raw chicken has touched it.

4   Lightly spray chicken nuggets with olive oil and bake for 8-10 minutes. Turn nuggets over and bake an additional 4-5 minutes or until cooked through.

Place 6 nuggets in large compartment with sealed containers of gluten-free BBQ sauce and gluten-free ketchup.

Nutrition Snapshot
Per serving: 308 calories, 4g fat, 0g saturated fat, 44g protein, 27g carbs, 3g fiber, 6g sugar, 142mg sodium

Sassy Seasoning Mix

Vegetarian
Gluten Free

2 Tbsp packed brown sugar
1 (2.2-oz) jar 21 Seasoning Salute or other seasoning blend

1   Place sugar and seasonings in a food processor and pulse for 3-4 minutes to pulverize.

2   Reserve remaining spice mixture in an airtight container and store in pantry.

Fingerling Potatoes

Vegetarian
Gluten Free

Kelly shared this quick and easy recipe with me. She learned it from her friend Guerin Barry, a wonderful actor who is also known for being able to whistle two notes at once – in harmony!

Prep Time 5 minutes
Cook Time approx. 20 minutes
Serves 4

1 lb fingerling potatoes
½ tsp salt
1 Tbsp no-salt seasoning blend, such as 21 Seasoning Salute

1 Rinse potatoes and place in a quart-size pot. Add water, just enough to cover potatoes.

2 Add salt and seasoning blend.

3 Bring to a boil over high heat. Do not cover.

4 When water comes to a boil, reduce heat to low, and simmer just long enough until water is completely gone. (Be sure to keep an eye on your potatoes so you don't cook them too long and burn them!)

Nutrition Snapshot
Per serving: 73 calories, 0g fat, 0g saturated fat, 2g protein, 20g carbs, 2g fiber, 2g sugar, 294mg sodium

Served here with: Mandarin orange wedges.

Kelly's Tip!

Turn any packed meal into a Happy Meal simply by including a surprise toy, a special note, or even coupons your child can trade in for some fun time with you.

It Mighta Choked Artie, but It Ain't Gonna Choke Me

I'm a huge fan of artichokes, but I always hated the amount of fat in the dips usually served with them (butter, mayonnaise...blech!) I decided to come up with a healthier version. This is one of my son's favorite recipes. He's asked me to write it down so that he can take it to college and impress the ladies!

Steamed Artichoke

Prep Time 10 minutes
Cook Time 20 minutes
Serves 4

4 whole artichokes

1 Fill a large pot with just enough water to cover bottom. Bring to a full boil over high heat. While water is heating, trim and discard the stems and tough outer leaves of artichokes.

2 When water is boiling, place steamer insert in pot and set artichokes in steamer, stem-side down. Cover pot with lid and allow artichokes to steam for approximately 20 minutes, or until tender.

3 Remove artichokes from pot and drain. Remove leaves until you get to the "heart." Reserve the heart for another dish, or include.

Salmon Tarragon

Prep Time 5 minutes
Cook Time 20 minutes
Serves 4

1 (12-oz) pkg frozen Wild Alaskan Sockeye Salmon Fillets, thawed
Juice of 1 orange
½ tsp dried tarragon

1 Preheat oven to 375° F. Place thawed salmon in Pyrex cooking dish sprayed with nonstick cooking spray, and pour orange juice over salmon. Sprinkle with tarragon. Bake for 20 minutes or until salmon is opaque in the center.

Place ¼ of salmon in large compartment along with artichoke leaves.

Tarragon Dip

¼ cup Dijon mustard
¼ cup tarragon vinegar
⅛ tsp dried tarragon

1 Mix Dijon mustard, tarragon vinegar, and dried tarragon until well incorporated. Pour in smaller compartment of EasyLunchbox.

Served here with: Pineapple chunks.

 **Kelly's Tip!**

Even if you don't have tarragon vinegar on hand, you'll want to give Lauri's wonderful dip a try. I had only rice vinegar in my pantry the day Loren brought home some huge artichokes from the farmers' market, so I used that. The dip was delicious, even with my vinegar substitution. Feel free to experiment with this and other recipes in this book: modify or adapt them to suit your tastes (or your pantry).

"Hell, there are no rules here --- we are trying to accomplish something." - Thomas A. Edison

Pack it Gluten-Free!

Laura Fuentes

As a mother of three, I want to feed my children wholesome fresh food. I have two picky eaters, so healthy lunches must be visually appealing and convenient to take on the go. At school, while other kids eat processed foods with unidentifiable ingredients, my children eat simple lunches that look like what their friends are eating, but are made with wholesome, fresh ingredients from my own kitchen.

Being a full-time working parent has taught me the importance of planning ahead and simplifying our lives, especially when it comes to food. As the CEO of MOMables™, a subscription based, school lunch menu-planning company for busy parents, I know the importance of feeding kids uncomplicated, yet nutritious food they will actually eat.

The following recipes are from our MOMables™ menus (MOMables.com). I hope you enjoy their simplicity, quick preparation, and delicious taste. You can follow my personal journey and my love for good food at Super Glue Mom (SuperGlueMom.com).

"I love that my mom is teaching me how to make our lunches. I feel good about my food and happy that my brother eats what I help make. I have the best school lunches and my friends look in my container every day to see what I have. They are yummy, and I know I'm special because she makes them just for me" - Daughter Sofia, 6

Salad You'll Swim Upstream For!

This twist on traditional tuna salad will satisfy the pickiest eaters. Loaded with good-for-you omega-3 fatty acids and protein, this gluten-free lunch will be one you'll make often. It goes perfectly on a green salad, between slices of gluten-free sandwich bread, or with a side of crackers.

Salmon Salad

Gluten Free

Prep Time 5 minutes
Serves 2

1 (7-oz) can salmon, drained, or cooked fresh salmon
1 ½ Tbsp mayonnaise or Greek yogurt
Juice of ½ lemon
⅛ tsp ground black pepper
¼ cup celery, finely chopped

1 Separate and crumble salmon into a bowl (checking for bones) and set aside.

2 In a bowl, combine mayonnaise, lemon juice, and pepper. Add to salmon. Toss in celery and stir to combine all ingredients.

3 Serve in large compartment on top of a few romaine lettuce leaves.

Nutrition Snapshot
Per serving: 186 calories, 10g fat, 2g saturated fat, 20g protein, 4g carbs, 0g fiber, 1g sugar, 638mg sodium

Served here with: Sliced veggies and gluten-free Pop Chips.

Kelly's Tip!

Feed your brain! Lots of evidence indicates that omega-3 fatty acids are particularly beneficial for brain health. Canned salmon has almost three times the amount of omega-3 oils as a can of tuna. Omega-3 oils may lower cholesterol, triglycerides, and blood pressure. Other fish high in omega-3 include mackerel, lake trout, herring, and sardines. Flaxseed and walnuts are also good sources for this healthy fat.

Did You Know?

The species of salmon (pink, chum, and sockeye) found in canned form are lower on the food chain than tuna, and therefore have fewer toxins. The salmon you find in canned salmon dined primarily on crustaceans and plankton; the tuna you find in canned tuna fed primarily on other fish.

Dip Dip Hooray!

Homemade Ranch dip mix is a great recipe to have in your kitchen arsenal. This mix can be used to make salad dressing, dip, or a coating for chicken or fish. It's versatile, easy to make, and inexpensive. You'll never buy the packets again! Mixed with Greek yogurt, it's the perfect high-protein lunch dip.

Homemade Ranch Dip

Prep Time 5 min
Serves 2

1 (6-oz) carton of plain Greek yogurt
2 tsp Laura's Spice Mix (recipe below)

1   Combine yogurt with spice mix. More spices can be added to taste.

Nutrition Snapshot
Per serving: 82 calories, 2g fat, 1g saturated fat, 9g protein, 7g carbs, 1g fiber, 5g sugar, 43mg sodium

Laura's Spice Mix

2 Tbsp dried parsley
1 tsp dried dill
1 tsp onion powder
½ tsp dried basil
¼ tsp black pepper
1 ½ tsp garlic powder

1   Combine all ingredients in a bowl.

2   For a smoother texture dip, pour spices into a coffee bean grinder and pulse for 15-20 seconds. One batch makes enough for about 3 cups of dip. Store remaining spices in airtight container.

Served here with: Lara Bar and cubed cheese.

Kelly's Tip! EasyLunchboxes are not leakproof and are not meant for use with liquids, but you can keep runnier foods, such as yogurt or applesauce, from leaking. Cut a square of wax paper that is larger than the compartment, and place it over that section before pushing the lid down securely. For salad dressings and other liquid sauces, include individual, leakproof sauce containers with your lunch.

Did You Know?

Ranch dressing was invented on a working ranch in California during the 1950s. The original recipe was a blend of spices, mixed with buttermilk and mayonnaise.

Pack it Gluten-Free!

Keeley McGuire

Being a mother with a full-time job and household to run makes for a busy life, but I view it all as an adventure. Our family is full of life, passion, faith, and sports. When we're not cheering on our favorite athletic teams, you can find my daughter, Little Miss, and me in the kitchen: baking, cooking, trying new recipes, and having fun. She's proud to be my little sous chef! Sharing time in the kitchen is great for bonding, and educational as well. I'm teaching her to read recipes, figure measurements, and use fractions.

My daughter drives my passion for packing healthy, fun lunches. She is a picky eater, and she has a severe peanut allergy. She cannot eat school-provided foods. Recently, she also began a gluten-free diet. Her fun and appealing lunches have inspired her to try new things and "good for me" foods. I take pride in knowing the foods I pack for her are healthy, are safe for her allergies, and make her feel special.

I share crafts, recipes, lunch box ideas, and my love of the slow cooker on my blog, Keeley McGuire (keeleymcguire.blogspot.com). I'm also a contributor to MOMables.com.

Something Sweet for my Sweetie

Sweet potatoes are delicious and packed full of vitamin A. Since starting my daughter on a gluten-free diet, we've been eating and experimenting with sweet potatoes more often. She loves their bright color; I love knowing she's getting added nutrition.

We like to bake these tasty muffins ahead of time and then keep a few in the refrigerator to eat later. They are easy to reheat. They make a great side dish at dinner or a delicious lunch box treat.

Sweet Potato Apple Cheese Muffins

Prep Time 10 minutes
Cook Time 25 minutes
Makes 12 muffins

Vegetarian
Gluten Free

1 ½ cups cooked, mashed sweet potatoes
2 medium size sweet-firm apples (Gala, Empire, or Rome)
1 Tbsp ground cinnamon
1 cup brown sugar
1 ½ tsp baking powder
1 cup gluten-free, all-purpose flour mix, or Just Almond Meal
1 large beaten egg
5 Tbsp organic unsweetened applesauce
1 cup sharp shredded cheddar cheese (other suggested cheese: Brie, Gouda, or goat)

1 Preheat oven to 350° F. Lightly grease 12-cup muffin pan.

2 Peel and core apples; dice apples into ¼-inch pieces.

3 In a large bowl, mix together the mashed sweet potatoes, apples, cinnamon, sugar, baking powder, and flour. Add egg and applesauce then mix to a smooth batter.

4 Pour batter into muffin pan, filling each cup completely. Bake for 20 minutes.

5 Remove from oven and top each muffin with cheese, evenly. Bake for 3-5 more minutes, until cheese has melted.

Nutrition Snapshot
Per muffin: 74 calories, 3g fat, 2g saturated fat, 3g protein, 8g carbs, 1g fiber, 1g sugar, 59mg sodium

Served here with: Gluten-free lunch meats and cheese slices, freshly peeled mandarin orange slices, and celery sticks with Sunflower Seed Butter.

Did You Know?

The sweet potato and the yam aren't even distantly related. The yam is grown in tropical climates such as South America, the Caribbean, and Africa, and the sweet potato is native to North Carolina. Certain kinds of sweet potatoes become soft and moist when cooked and have the texture of a cooked yam, so early Americans from other countries (where the yam was popular) began to using the terms "yam" and "sweet potato" interchangeably.

The Apple Doesn't Fall Far From the Cornbread

Growing up, I remember what a special treat it was when my mom would buy us corn dogs. I marveled at the concept of eating a breaded dog on a stick.

Fast forward to my own daughter, who finds anything in the shape of a cupcake or muffin to be equally captivating. These chicken-apple sausage and cornbread muffins are an easy bake. We make them on the weekends, keeping a few in the refrigerator to be easily reheated for lunches. The rest go in the freezer so I can pull them out as needed. These are my favorite kind of lunch box food: homemade, at my fingertips, and delicious.

Chicken Apple Sausage Cornbread

Gluten Free

Prep Time 10 minutes
Cook Time 25 minutes
Makes 12 muffins

1 cup corn meal or Polenta Corn Grits
1 cup gluten-free, all-purpose flour mix, or Just Almond Meal
2 medium size sweet-firm apples (Gala, Empire, or Rome)
2 links Chicken Apple Sausage
1 cup milk
½ tsp baking soda
2 large beaten eggs
½ cup softened butter
5 tsp honey, divided

1 Preheat oven to 350° F. Lightly grease 12-cup muffin pan.

2 Peel and core apples; dice apples into ¼- to ½-inch pieces.

3 On a cutting board, dice the sausage into small, bite-size pieces.

4 In a large bowl, mix together the corn meal, flour, milk, baking soda, eggs, and butter. Add sausage, apples, and 3 tsp honey; mix well.

5 Pour sausage mixture into muffin pan, filling each cup. Bake for 20-25 minutes, until muffins rise and turn golden in color. Remove from oven and drizzle with remaining honey. Place muffins in large compartment surrounded by fresh salad greens. Don't forget to include a small container of your favorite gluten-free salad dressing!

Nutrition Snapshot
Per muffin: 89 calories, 8g fat, 5g saturated fat, 1g protein, 2g carbs, 0g fiber, 2g sugar, 13mg sodium

Served here with: Pears, apple slices, and yogurt.

Did You Know?

Corn originated in the United States, and you can find it in the form of polenta at many Mexican restaurants. The word "polenta" originated in Italy to refer to a porridge made of grain.

Cauli-fornia Dreamin' Pizza

What kid, or adult for that matter, doesn't love pizza? I think my daughter would eat it every day, if I let her. Gluten-free pre-made crusts can be expensive, so I opt for a healthier do-it-yourself version made from cauliflower. It's not only delicious, it's lower in calories than typical crusts. These lunch-box-size pizzas are sure to be a hit with the whole family.

Cauliflower Crust Pizza

Gluten Free
Vegetarian

Omit chicken and bacon bits or substitute with vegetarian alternative meats and bacon

Prep Time 5 minutes
Cook Time 30 minutes
Serves 2

Crust Ingredients:
¾ of a whole head cauliflower (about 3 cups cauliflower florets)
½ a large beaten egg
1 tsp garlic salt w/ parsley seasoning, or 21 Seasoning Salute with pinch of salt
½ tsp Italian Herb (grinder) seasoning
½ cup shredded mozzarella cheese

Toppings:
3-4 tsp pizza sauce
½ cup shredded mozzarella cheese
½ cup grilled chicken strips, diced
2 tsp gluten-free bacon bits & pieces

1 Preheat oven to 400° F. Meanwhile, place cauliflower florets in a food processor and process to a "flour"-like texture.

2 Microwave processed cauliflower in a microwave safe bowl on high for 5 minutes.

3 Add egg, seasoning, and cheese to cauliflower and mix until fully incorporated.

4 Form mixture into pizza crusts approximately 4.5 inches in diameter and place on baking sheet lined with parchment paper. Lightly coat each "crust" with cooking spray and place in oven, bake for 15-20 minutes.

5 Remove from oven and top with pizza sauce, cheese, grilled chicken, and bacon bits.

6 Return to oven and broil until cheese is melted, approximately 5 minutes.

Nutrition Snapshot
Per serving: 327 calories, 13g fat, 7g saturated fat, 36g protein, 18g carbs, 7g fiber, 8g sugar, 1248mg sodium

Served here with: Red seedless grapes, Freeze Dried Bananas, and baby spinach salad with broccoli slaw mix.

Did You Know?

Cauliflower is sold in a variety of colors besides the standard white. It can be green, orange, brown, purple, or yellow (When they invent red and blue cauliflower, the rainbow will be complete.) Cauliflower is from the same family of vegetables as cabbage, Brussels sprouts, kale, broccoli, and collard greens.

Recipe Index

Want More?
Additional TJ's recipes and packed lunch pics gathered from the EasyLunchboxes community!
easylunchboxes.com/trader-joes-book

Photo Credits

TJ Store Locations

Arizona

Ahwatukee # 177
4025 E. Chandler Blvd., Ste. 38
Ahwatukee, AZ 85048
Phone: 480-759-2295

Glendale # 085
7720 West Bell Road
Glendale, AZ 85308
Phone: 623-776-7414

Mesa # 089
2050 East Baseline Rd.
Mesa, AZ 85204
Phone: 480-632-0951

Paradise Valley # 282
4726 E. Shea Blvd.
Phoenix, AZ 85028
Phone: 602-485-7788

**Phoenix
(Town & Country) # 090**
4821 N. 20th Street
Phoenix, AZ 85016
Phone: 602-912-9022

Prescott
252 Lee Blvd
Prescott, AZ 86303
Phone: 928-443-9075

Scottsdale (North) # 087
7555 E. Frank Lloyd Wright
N. Scottsdale, AZ 85260
Phone: 480-367-8920

Scottsdale # 094
6202 N. Scottsdale Road
Scottsdale, AZ 85253
Phone: 480-948-9886

Surprise # 092
14095 West Grand Ave.
Surprise, AZ 85374
Phone: 623-546-1640

Tempe # 093
6460 S. McClintock Drive
Tempe, AZ 85283
Phone: 480-838-4142

**Tucson
(Crossroads) # 088**
4766 East Grant Road
Tucson, AZ 85712
Phone: 520-323-4500

**Tucson (Wilmot &
Speedway)# 095**
1101 N. Wilmot Rd.
Suite #147
Tucson, AZ 85712
Phone: 520-733-1313

**Tucson (Campbell &
Limberlost) # 191**
4209 N. Campbell Ave.
Tucson, AZ 85719
Phone: 520-325-0069

Tucson - Oro Valley # 096
7912 N. Oracle
Oro Valley, AZ 85704
Phone: 520-797-4207

California

Agoura Hills
28941 Canwood Street
Agoura Hills, CA 91301
Phone: 818-865-8217

Alameda # 109
2217 South Shore Center
Alameda, CA 94501
Phone: 510-769-5450

Aliso Viejo # 195
The Commons
26541 Aliso Creek Road
Aliso Viejo, CA 92656
Phone: 949-643-5531

Arroyo Grande # 117
955 Rancho Parkway
Arroyo Grande, CA 93420
Phone: 805-474-6114

Bakersfield # 014
8200-C 21 Stockdale Hwy.
Bakersfield, CA 93311
Phone: 661-837-8863

Berkeley #186
1885 University Ave.
Berkeley, CA 94703
Phone: 510-204-9074

Bixby Knolls # 116
4121 Atlantic Ave.
Bixby Knolls, CA 90807
Phone: 562-988-0695

Brea # 011
2500 E. Imperial Hwy.
Suite 177
Brea, CA 92821
Phone 714-257-1180

Brentwood # 201
5451 Lone Tree Way
Brentwood, CA 94513
Phone: 925-516-3044

Burbank # 124
214 East Alameda
Burbank, CA 91502
Phone: 818-848-4299

Camarillo # 114
363 Carmen Drive
Camarillo, CA 93010
Phone: 805-388-1925

Campbell # 073
1875 Bascom Avenue
Campbell, CA 95008
Phone: 408-369-7823

Capitola # 064
3555 Clares Street #D
Capitola, CA 95010
Phone: 831-464-0115

Carlsbad # 220
2629 Gateway Road
Carlsbad, CA 92009
Phone: 760-603-8473

Castro Valley # 084
22224 Redwood Road
Castro Valley, CA 94546
Phone: 510-538-2738

Cathedral City # 118
67-720 East Palm Cyn.
Cathedral City, CA 92234
Phone: 760-202-0090

Cerritos # 104
12861 Towne Center Drive
Cerritos, CA 90703
Phone: 562-402-5148

Chatsworth # 184
10330 Mason Ave.
Chatsworth, CA 91311
Phone: 818-341-3010

Chico # 199
801 East Ave., Suite #110
Chico, CA 95926
Phone: 530-343-9920

Chino Hills # 216
13911 Peyton Dr.
Chino Hills, CA 91709
Phone: 909-627-1404

Chula Vista # 120
878 Eastlake Parkway,
Suite 810
Chula Vista, CA 91914
Phone: 619-656-5370

Claremont # 214
475 W. Foothill Blvd.
Claremont, CA 91711
Phone: 909-625-8784

Clovis # 180
1077 N. Willow, Suite 101
Clovis, CA 93611
Phone: 559-325-3120

**Concord (Oak Grove
& Treat) # 083**
785 Oak Grove Road
Concord, CA 94518
Phone: 925-521-1134

Concord (Airport) # 060
1150 Concord Ave.
Concord, CA 94520
Phone: 925-689-2990

Corona # 213
2790 Cabot Drive, Ste. 165
Corona, CA 92883
Phone: 951-603-0299

Costa Mesa # 035
640 W. 17th Street
Costa Mesa, CA 92627
Phone: 949-642-5134

Culver City # 036
9290 Culver Blvd.
Culver City, CA 90232
Phone: 310-202-1108

Daly City # 074
417 Westlake Center
Daly City, CA 94015
Phone: 650-755-3825

Danville # 065
85 Railroad Ave.
Danville, CA 94526
Phone: 925-838-5757

Davis
885 Russell Blvd.
Davis, CA 95616
Phone: 530-757-2693

Eagle Rock # 055
1566 Colorado Blvd.
Eagle Rock, CA 90041
Phone: 323-257-6422

El Cerrito # 108
225 El Cerrito Plaza
El Cerrito, CA 94530
Phone: 510-524-7609

Elk Grove # 190
9670 Bruceville Road
Elk Grove, CA 95757
Phone: 916-686-9980

Emeryville # 072
5700 Christie Avenue
Emeryville, CA 94608
Phone: 510-658-8091

Encinitas # 025
115 N. El Camino Real,
Suite A
Encinitas, CA 92024
Phone: 760-634-2114

Encino # 056
17640 Burbank Blvd.
Encino, CA 91316
Phone: 818-990-7751

Escondido # 105
1885 So. Centre City
Pkwy., Unit "A"
Escondido, CA 92025
Phone: 760-233-4020

Fair Oaks # 071
5309 Sunrise Ave.
Fair Oaks, CA 95628
Phone: 916-863-1744

Fairfield # 101
1350 Gateway Blvd.,
Suite A1-A7
Fairfield, CA 94533
Phone: 707-434-0144

Folsom # 172
850 East Bidwell
Folsom, CA 95630
Phone: 916-817-8820

Fremont # 077
39324 Argonaut Way
Fremont, CA 94538
Phone: 510-794-1386

Fresno # 008
5376 N. Blackstone
Fresno, CA 93710
Phone: 559-222-4348

Glendale # 053
130 N. Glendale Ave.
Glendale, CA 91206
Phone: 818-637-2990

Goleta # 110
5767 Calle Real
Goleta, CA 93117
Phone: 805-692-2234

Granada Hills # 044
11114 Balboa Blvd.
Granada Hills, CA 91344
Phone: 818-368-6461

Hollywood
1600 N. Vine Street
Los Angeles, CA 90028
Phone: 323-856-0689

Huntington Bch. # 047
18681-101 Main Street
Huntington Bch., CA 92648
Phone: 714-848-9640

Huntington Bch. # 241
21431 Brookhurst St.
Huntington Bch., CA 92646
Phone: 714-968-4070

Huntington Harbor # 244
Huntington Harbour Mall
16821 Algonquin St.
Huntington Bch., CA 92649
Phone: 714-846-7307

**Irvine (Walnut Village
Center) # 037**
14443 Culver Drive
Irvine, CA 92604
Phone: 949-857-8108

**Irvine (University
Center) # 111**
4225 Campus Dr.
Irvine, CA 92612
Phone: 949-509-6138

**Irvine (Irvine &
Sand Cyn) # 210**
6222 Irvine Blvd.
Irvine, CA 92620
Phone: 949-551-6402

La Cañada # 042
475 Foothill Blvd.
La Canada, CA 91011
Phone: 818-790-6373

La Quinta # 189
46-400 Washington Street
La Quinta, CA 92253
Phone: 760-777-1553

Lafayette # 115
3649 Mt. Diablo Blvd.
Lafayette, CA 94549
Phone: 925-299-9344

Laguna Hills # 039
24321 Avenue De La Carlota
Laguna Hills, CA 92653
Phone: 949-586-8453

Laguna Niguel # 103
32351 Street of the Golden
Lantern
Laguna Niguel, CA 92677
Phone: 949-493-8599

La Jolla # 020
8657 Villa LaJolla
Drive #210
La Jolla, CA 92037
Phone: 858-546-8629

La Mesa # 024
5495 Grossmont Center Dr.
La Mesa, CA 91942
Phone: 619-466-0105

Larkspur # 235
2052 Redwood Hwy
Larkspur, CA 94921
Phone: 415-945-7955

Livermore # 208
1122-A East Stanley Blvd.
Livermore, CA 94550
Phone: 925-243-1947

Long Beach (PCH) # 043
6451 E. Pacific Coast Hwy.
Long Beach, CA 90803
Phone: 562-596-4388

**Long Beach
(Bellflower Blvd.) # 194**
2222 Bellflower Blvd.
Long Beach, CA 90815
Phone: 562-596-2514

Los Altos # 127
2310 Homestead Rd.
Los Altos, CA 94024
Phone: 408-245-1917

**Los Angeles
(Silver Lake) # 017**
2738 Hyperion Ave.
Los Angeles, CA 90027
Phone: 323-665-6774

Los Angeles # 031
263 S. La Brea
Los Angeles, CA 90036
Phone: 323-965-1989

**Los Angeles
(Sunset Strip) # 192**
8000 Sunset Blvd.
Los Angeles, CA 90046
Phone: 323-822-7663

Los Gatos # 181
15466 Los Gatos Blvd.
Los Gatos, CA 95032
Phone 408-356-2324

Los Angeles (3rd & Fairfax)
W 3rd St. & S Fairfax Ave
Los Angeles, CA 90048
Phone: 323-931-4012

Manhattan Beach # 034
1821 Manhattan
Beach. Blvd.
Manhattan Bch., CA 90266
Phone: 310-372-1274

Manhattan Beach # 196
1800 Rosecrans Blvd.
Manhattan Beach,
CA 90266
Phone: 310-725-9800

Menlo Park # 069
720 Menlo Avenue
Menlo Park, CA 94025
Phone: 650-323-2134

Millbrae # 170
765 Broadway
Millbrae, CA 94030
Phone: 650-259-9142

Mission Viejo # 126
25410 Marguerite Parkway
Mission Viejo, CA 92692
Phone: 949-581-5638

Modesto # 009
3250 Dale Road
Modesto, CA 95356
Phone: 209-491-0445

Monrovia # 112
604 W. Huntington Dr.
Monrovia, CA 91016
Phone: 626-358-8884

Monterey # 204
570 Munras Ave., Ste. 20
Monterey, CA 93940
Phone: 831-372-2010

Montrose
2462 Honolulu Ave.
Montrose, CA 91020
Phone: 818-957-3613

Morgan Hill # 202
17035 Laurel Road
Morgan Hill, CA 95037
Phone: 408-778-6409

Mountain View # 081
590 Showers Dr.
Mountain View, CA 94040
Phone: 650-917-1013

Napa # 128
3654 Bel Aire Plaza
Napa, CA 94558
Phone: 707-256-0806

Newbury Park # 243
125 N. Reino Road
Newbury Park, CA
Phone: 805-375-1984

Newport Beach # 125
8086 East Coast Highway
Newport Beach, CA 92657
Phone: 949-494-7404

Novato # 198
7514 Redwood Blvd.
Novato, CA 94945
Phone: 415-898-9359

**Oakland
(Lakeshore) # 203**
3250 Lakeshore Ave.
Oakland, CA 94610
Phone: 510-238-9076

Oakland (Rockridge) # 231
5727 College Ave.
Oakland, CA 94618
Phone: 510-923-9428

Oceanside # 22
2570 Vista Way
Oceanside, CA 92054
Phone: 760-433-9994

Orange # 046
2114 N. Tustin St.
Orange, CA 92865
Phone: 714-283-5697

Pacific Grove # 008
1170 Forest Avenue
Pacific Grove, CA 93950
Phone: 831-656-0180

Palm Desert # 003
44-250 Town Center Way,
Suite C6
Palm Desert, CA 92260
Phone: 760-340-2291

Palmdale # 185
39507 10th Street West
Palmdale, CA 93551
Phone: 661-947-2890

Palo Alto # 207
855 El Camino Real
Palo Alto, CA 94301
Phone: 650-327-7018

**Pasadena
(S. Lake Ave.) # 179**
345 South Lake Ave.
Pasadena, CA 91101
Phone: 626-395-9553

**Pasadena
(S. Arroyo Pkwy.) # 051**
610 S. Arroyo Parkway
Pasadena, CA 91105
Phone: 626-568-9254

**Pasadena
(Hastings Ranch) # 171**
467 Rosemead Blvd.
Pasadena, CA 91107
Phone: 626-351-3399

Petaluma # 107
169 North McDowell Blvd.
Petaluma, CA 94954
Phone: 707-769-2782

Pinole # 230
2742 Pinole Valley Rd.
Pinole, CA 94564
Phone: 510-222-3501

Pleasanton # 066
4040 Pimlico #150
Pleasanton, CA 94588
Phone: 925-225-3600

Rancho Cucamonga # 217
6401 Haven Ave.
Rancho Cucamonga,
CA 91737
Phone: 909-476-1410

Rancho Palos Verdes # 057
28901 S. Western Ave. #243
Rancho Palos Verdes,
CA 90275
Phone: 310-832-1241

Rancho Palos Verdes # 233
31176 Hawthorne Blvd.
Rancho Palos Verdes, CA 90275
Phone: 310-544-1727

Rancho Santa
Margarita # 027
30652 Santa Margarita Pkwy.
Suite F102
Rancho Santa Margarita,
CA 92688
Phone: 949-888-3640

Redding # 219
845 Browning St.
Redding, CA 96003
Phone: 530-223-4875

Redlands # 099
552 Orange Street Plaza
Redlands, CA 92374
Phone: 909-798-3888

Redondo Beach # 038
1761 S. Elena Avenue
Redondo Bch., CA 90277
Phone: 310-316-1745

Riverside # 15
6225 Riverside Plaza
Riverside, CA 92506
Phone: 951-682-4684

Roseville # 80
1117 Roseville Square
Roseville, CA 95678
Phone: 916-784-9084

Sacramento
(Folsom Blvd.) # 175
5000 Folsom Blvd.
Sacramento, CA 95819
Phone: 916-456-1853

Sacramento
(Fulton & Marconi) # 070
2625 Marconi Avenue
Sacramento, CA 95821
Phone: 916-481-8797

San Carlos # 174
1482 El Camino Real
San Carlos, CA 94070
Phone: 650-594-2138

San Clemente # 016
638 Camino DeLosMares,
Sp.#115-G
San Clemente, CA 92673
Phone: 949-240-9996

San Diego
(Hillcrest) # 026
1090 University Ste.
G100-107
San Diego, CA 92103
Phone: 619-296-3122

San Diego
(Point Loma) # 188
2401 Truxtun Rd., Ste. 300
San Diego, CA 92106
Phone: 619-758-9272

San Diego
(Pacific Beach) # 021
1211 Garnet Avenue
San Diego, CA 92109
Phone: 858-272-7235

San Diego (Carmel
Mtn. Ranch) # 023
11955 Carmel Mtn. Rd. #702
San Diego, CA 92128
Phone: 858-673-0526

San Diego
(Scripps Ranch) # 221
9850 Hibert Street
San Diego, CA 92131
Phone: 858-549-9185

San Dimas # 028
856 Arrow Hwy. "C"
Target Center
San Dimas, CA 91773
Phone: 909-305-4757

San Francisco
(9th Street) # 078
555 9th Street
San Francisco, CA 94103
Phone: 415-863-1292

San Francisco
(Masonic Ave.) # 100
3 Masonic Avenue
San Francisco, CA 94118
Phone: 415-346-9964

San Francisco
(North Beach) # 019
401 Bay Street
San Francisco, CA 94133
Phone: 415-351-1013

San Francisco
(Stonestown) # 236
265 Winston Dr.
San Francisco, CA 94132
Phone: 415-665-1835

San Gabriel # 032
7260 N. Rosemead Blvd.
San Gabriel, CA 91775
Phone: 626-285-5862

San Jose (Bollinger) # 232
7250 Bollinger Rd.
San Jose, CA 95129
Phone: 408-873-7384

San Jose
(Coleman Ave) # 212
635 Coleman Ave.
San Jose, CA 95110
Phone: 408-298-9731

San Jose
(Old Almaden) # 063
5353 Almaden Expressway
#J-38
San Jose, CA 95118
Phone: 408-927-9091

San Jose
(Westgate West) # 062
5269 Prospect
San Jose, CA 95129
Phone: 408-446-5055

San Luis Obispo # 041
3977 Higuera Street
San Luis Obispo, CA 93401
Phone: 805-783-2780

San Mateo
(Grant Street) # 067
1820-22 S. Grant Street
San Mateo, CA 94402
Phone: 650-570-6140

San Mateo
(Hillsdale) # 245
45 W Hillsdale Blvd
San Mateo, CA 94403
Phone: 650-286-1509

San Rafael # 061
337 Third Street
San Rafael, CA 94901
Phone: 415-454-9530

Santa Ana # 113
3329 South Bristol Street
Santa Ana, CA 92704
Phone: 714-424-9304

Santa Barbara
(S. Milpas St.) # 059
29 S. Milpas Street
Santa Barbara, CA 93103
Phone: 805-564-7878

Santa Barbara
(De La Vina) # 183
3025 De La Vina
Santa Barbara, CA 93105
Phone: 805-563-7383

Santa Cruz # 193
700 Front Street
Santa Cruz, CA 95060
Phone: 831-425-0140

Santa Maria # 239
1303 S. Bradley Road
Santa Maria, CA 93454
Phone: 805-925-1657

Santa Monica # 006
3212 Pico Blvd.
Santa Monica, CA 90405
Phone: 310-581-0253

Santa Rosa
(Cleveland Ave.) # 075
3225 Cleveland Avenue
Santa Rosa, CA 95403
Phone: 707-525-1406

Santa Rosa
(Santa Rosa Ave.) # 178
2100 Santa Rosa Ave.
Santa Rosa, CA 95407
Phone: 707-535-0788

Sherman Oaks # 049
14119 Riverside Drive
Sherman Oaks, CA 91423
Phone: 818-789-2771

Simi Valley # 030
2975-A Cochran St.
Simi Valley, CA 93065
Phone: 805-520-3135

South Pasadena # 018
613 Mission Street
South Pasadena, CA 91030
Phone: 626-441-6263

South San Francisco # 187
301 McLellan Dr.
So. San Francisco,
CA 94080
Phone: 650-583-6401

Stockton # 076
6535 Pacific Avenue
Stockton, CA 95207
Phone: 209-951-7597

Studio City # 122
11976 Ventura Blvd.
Studio City, CA 91604
Phone: 818-509-0168

Sunnyvale # 068
727 Sunnyvale/
Saratoga Rd.
Sunnyvale, CA 94087
Phone: 408-481-9082

Temecula # 102
40665 Winchester Rd., Bldg. B,
Ste. 4-6
Temecula, CA 92591
Phone: 951-296-9964

Templeton # 211
1111 Rossi Road
Templeton, CA 93465
Phone: 805-434-9562

Thousand Oaks # 196
451 Avenida
De Los Arboles
Thousand Oaks, CA 91360
Phone: 805-492-7107

Toluca Lake # 054
10130 Riverside Drive
Toluca Lake, CA 91602
Phone: 818-762-2787

Torrance
(Hawthorne Blvd.) # 121
19720 Hawthorne Blvd.
Torrance, CA 90503
Phone: 310-793-8585

Torrance (Rolling
Hills Plaza) # 029
2545 Pacific Coast Highway
Torrance, CA 90505
Phone: 310-326-9520

Tustin # 197
12932 Newport Avenue
Tustin, CA 92780
Phone: 714-669-3752

Upland # 010
333 So. Mountain Avenue
Upland, CA 91786
Phone: 909-946-4799

Valencia # 013
26517 Bouquet Canyon Rd
Santa Clarita, CA 91350
Phone: 661-263-3796

Ventura # 045
1795 S. Victoria Avenue
Ventura, CA 93003
Phone: 805-650-9977

Ventura – Midtown
103 S. Mills Road Suite 104
Ventura, CA 93003
Phone: 805-658-2664

Walnut Creek # 123
1372 So. California Blvd.
Walnut Creek, CA 94596
Phone: 925-945-1674

West Hills # 050
6751 Fallbrook Ave.
West Hills, CA 91307
Phone: 818-347-2591

West Hollywood # 040
7304 Santa Monica Blvd.
West Hollywood, CA 90046
Phone: 323-851-9772

West Hollywood # 173
8611 Santa Monica Blvd.
West Hollywood, CA 90069
Phone: 310-657-0152

**West Los Angeles
(National Blvd.) # 007**
10850 National Blvd.
West Los Angeles, CA 90064
Phone: 310-470-1917

**West Los Angeles
S. Sepulveda Blvd.) # 119**
3456 S. Sepulveda Blvd.
West Los Angeles, CA 90034
Phone: 310-836-2458

**West Los Angeles
(Olympic) # 215**
11755 W. Olympic Blvd.
West Los Angeles,
CA 90064
Phone: 310-477-5949

Westchester # 033
8645 S. Sepulveda
Westchester, CA 90045
Phone: 310-338-9238

Westlake Village # 058
3835 E. Thousand
Oaks Blvd.
Westlake Village, CA 91362
Phone: 805-494-5040

Westwood # 234
1000 Glendon Avenue
Los Angeles, CA 90024
Phone: 310-824-1495

Whittier # 048
15025 E. Whittier Blvd.
Whittier, CA 90603
Phone: 562-698-1642

Woodland Hills # 209
21054 Clarendon St.
Woodland Hills, CA 91364
Phone: 818-712-9475

Yorba Linda # 176
19655 Yorba Linda Blvd.
Yorba Linda, CA 92886
Phone: 714-970-0116

Connecticut

Danbury # 525
113 Mill Plain Rd.
Danbury, CT 06811
Phone: 203-739-0098
Alcohol: Beer Only

Darien # 522
436 Boston Post Rd.
Darien, CT 06820
Phone: 203-656-1414
Alcohol: Beer Only

Fairfield # 523
2258 Black Rock Turnpike
Fairfield, CT 06825
Phone: 203-330-8301
Alcohol: Beer Only

Orange # 524
560 Boston Post Road
Orange, CT 06477
Phone: 203-795-5505
Alcohol: Beer Only

West Hartford # 526
1489 New Britain Ave.
West Hartford, CT 06110
Phone: 860-561-4771
Alcohol: Beer Only

Westport # 521
400 Post Road East
Westport, CT 06880
Phone: 203-226-8966
Alcohol: Beer Only

Delaware

Wilmington* # 536
5605 Concord Pike
Wilmington, DE 19803
Phone: 302-478-8494

District of Columbia

Washington # 653
1101 25th Street NW
Washington, DC 20037
Phone: 202-296-1921

Florida

Naples
10600 Tamiami Trail North
Naples, FL 34108
Phone: 239-596-5631

Sarasota – Coming Soon!
4101 S. Tamiami Trail
Sarasota, FL 34231
Phone: TBD

Georgia

Athens
1850 Epps Bridge Parkway
Athens, GA 30606
Phone: 706-583-8934

**Atlanta
(Buckhead) # 735**
3183 Peachtree Rd NE
Atlanta, GA 30305
Phone: 404-842-0907

Atlanta (Midtown) # 730
931 Monroe Dr., NE
Atlanta, GA 30308
Phone: 404-815-9210

Marietta # 732
4250 Roswell Road
Marietta, GA 30062
Phone: 678-560-3585

Norcross # 734
5185 Peachtree Parkway, Bld.
1200
Norcross, GA 30092
Phone: 678-966-9236

Roswell # 733
635 W. Crossville Road
Roswell, GA 30075
Phone: 770-645-8505

Sandy Springs # 731
6277 Roswell Road NE
Sandy Springs, GA 30328
Phone: 404-236-2414

Illinois

Algonquin # 699
1800 South Randall Road
Algonquin, IL 60102
Phone: 847-854-4886

Arlington Heights # 687
17 W. Rand Road
Arlington Heights, IL 60004
Phone: 847-506-0752

Batavia # 689
1942 West Fabyan
Parkway #222
Batavia, IL 60510
Phone: 630-879-3234

Chicago (Diversey Pkwy)
667 W. Diversey Pkwy
Chicago, IL 60614
Phone: 773-935-7255

**Chicago
(Lincoln & Grace) # 688**
3745 North Lincoln Avenue
Chicago, IL 60613
Phone: 773-248-4920

**Chicago
(Lincoln Park) # 691**
1840 North Clybourn
Avenue #200
Chicago, IL 60614
Phone: 312-274-9733

**Chicago
(River North) # 696**
44 E. Ontario St.
Chicago, IL 60611
Phone: 312-951-6369

Chicago (South Loop)
1147 S. Wabash Ave.
Chicago, IL 60605
Phone: 312-588-0489

Downers Grove # 683
122 Ogden Ave.
Downers Grove, IL 60515
Phone: 630-241-1662

Glen Ellyn # 680
680 Roosevelt Rd.
Glen Ellyn, IL 60137
Phone: 630-858-5077

Glenview # 681
1407 Waukegan Road
Glenview, IL 60025
Phone: 847-657-7821

La Grange # 685
25 North La Grange Road
La Grange, IL 60525
Phone: 708-579-0838

Lake Zurich # 684
735 W. Route 22**
Lake Zurich, IL 60047
Phone: 847-550-7827
[**For accurate driving
directions using
GPS, please use
735 W Main Street]

Naperville # 690
44 West Gartner Road
Naperville, IL 60540
Phone: 630-355-4389

Northbrook # 682
127 Skokie Blvd.
Northbrook, IL 60062
Phone: 847-498-9076

Oak Park # 697
483 N. Harlem Ave.
Oak Park, IL 60301
Phone: 708-386-1169

Orland Park # 686
14924 S. La Grange Road
Orland Park, IL 60462
Phone: 708-349-9021

Park Ridge # 698
190 North Northwest Hwy
Park Ridge, IL 60068
Phone: 847-292-1108

Indiana

**Indianapolis
(Castleton) # 671**
5473 East 82nd Street
Indianapolis, IN 46250
Phone: 317-595-8950

**Indianapolis
(West 86th) # 670**
2902 West 86th Street
Indianapolis, IN 46268
Phone: 317-337-1880

Iowa

West Des Moines
6305 Mills Civic Parkway
West Des Moines, IA 50266
Phone: 515-225-3820

Kansas

Leawood* #723
4201 W 119th Street
Leawood, KS 66209
Phone: 913-327-7209

Kentucky

Louisville
4600 Shelbyville Road
Louisville, KY 40207
Phone: 502-895-1361

Lexington Grocery
2326 Nicholasville Rd
Lexington, KY 40503
Phone: 859-313-5030

Lexington Wine
2320 Nicholasville Rd
Lexington, KY 40503
Phone: 859-277-0144

Maine

Portland # 519
87 Marginal Way
Portland, ME 04101
Phone: 207-699-3799

Store does not carry alcohol.

Maryland

Annapolis* # 650
160 F Jennifer Road
Annapolis, MD 21401
Phone: 410-573-0505

Bethesda* # 645
6831 Wisconsin Avenue
Bethesda, MD 20815
Phone: 301-907-0982

Columbia* # 658
6610 Marie Curie Dr.
(Int. of 175 & 108)
Elkridge, MD 21075
Phone: 410-953-8139

Gaithersburg* # 648
18270 Contour Rd.
Gaithersburg, MD 20877
Phone: 301-947-5953

Pikesville* # 655
1809 Reisterstown Road,
Suite #121
Pikesville, MD 21208
Phone: 410-484-8373

Rockville* # 642
12268-H Rockville Pike
Rockville, MD 20852
Phone: 301-468-6656

Silver Spring* # 652
10741 Columbia Pike
Silver Spring, MD 20901
Phone: 301-681-1675

Towson* # 649
1 E. Joppa Rd.
Towson, MD 21286
Phone: 410-296-9851

Massachusetts

Acton* # 511
145 Great Road
Acton, MA 01720
Phone: 978-266-8908

Arlington* # 505
1427 Massachusetts Ave.
Arlington, MA 02476
Phone: 781-646-9138

Boston #510
899 Boylston Street
Boston, MA 02115
Phone: 617-262-6505

Brookline # 501
1317 Beacon Street
Brookline, MA 02446
Phone: 617-278-9997

Burlington* # 515
51 Middlesex Turnpike
Burlington, MA 01803
Phone: 781-273-2310

Cambridge
748 Memorial Drive
Cambridge, MA 02139
Phone: 617-491-8582

**Cambridge
(Fresh Pond)* # 517**
211 Alewife Brook Pkwy
Cambridge, MA 02138
Phone: 617-498-3201

Framingham # 503
659 Worcester Road
Framingham, MA 01701
Phone: 508-935-2931

Hadley* # 512
375 Russell Street
Hadley, MA 01035
Phone: 413-587-3260

Hanover* # 513
1775 Washington Street
Hanover, MA 02339
Phone: 781-826-5389

Hyannis* # 514
Christmas Tree Promenade
655 Route 132, Unit 4-A
Hyannis, MA 02601
Phone: 508-790-3008

Needham Hts* 504
958 Highland Avenue
Needham Hts, MA 02494
Phone: 781-449-6993

Peabody* # 516
300 Andover Street,
Suite 15
Peabody, MA 01960
Phone: 978-977-5316

Saugus* # 506
358 Broadway, Unit B
(Shops @ Saugus, Rte. 1)
Saugus, MA 01906
Phone: 781-231-0369

Shrewsbury* # 508
77 Boston Turnpike
Shrewsbury, MA 01545
Phone: 508-755-9560

Tyngsboro* # 507
440 Middlesex Road
Tyngsboro, MA 01879
Phone: 978-649-2726

West Newton* # 509
1121 Washington St.
West Newton, MA 02465
Phone: 617-244-1620

Michigan

Ann Arbor # 678
2398 East Stadium Blvd.
Ann Arbor, MI 48104
Phone: 734-975-2455

Farmington Hills # 675
31221 West 14 Mile Road
Farmington Hills, MI 48334
Phone: 248-737-4609

Grosse Pointe # 665
17028 Kercheval Ave.
Grosse Pointe, MI 48230
Phone: 313-640-7794

Northville # 667
20490 Haggerty Road
Northville, MI 48167
Phone: 734-464-3675

Rochester Hills # 668
3044 Walton Blvd.
Rochester Hills, MI 48309
Phone: 248-375-2190

Royal Oak # 674
27880 Woodward Ave.
Royal Oak, MI 48067
Phone: 248-582-9002

Minnesota

Maple Grove # 713
12105 Elm Creek Blvd. N.
Maple Grove, MN 55369
Phone: 763-315-1739

Minnetonka # 714
11220 Wayzata Blvd
Minnetonka, MN 55305
Phone: 952-417-9080

Rochester
1200 16th St. SW
Rochester, NY 55902
Phone: 952-417-9080

St. Louis Park # 710
4500 Excelsior Blvd.
St. Louis Park, MN 55416
Phone: 952-285-1053

St. Paul # 716
484 Lexington Parkway S.
St. Paul, MN 55116
Phone: 651-698-3119

Woodbury # 715
8960 Hudson Road
Woodbury, MN 55125
Phone: 651-735-0269

Missouri

Brentwood # 792
48 Brentwood
Promenade Court
Brentwood, MO 63144
Phone: 314-963-0253

Chesterfield # 693
1679 Clarkson Road
Chesterfield, MO 63017
Phone: 636-536-7846

Creve Coeur # 694
11505 Olive Blvd.
Creve Coeur, MO 63141
Phone: 314-569-0427

Des Peres # 695
13343 Manchester Rd.
Des Peres, MO 63131
Phone: 314-984-5051

Kansas City
8600 Ward Parkway
Kansas City, MO 64114
Phone: 816-333-5322

Nebraska

Lincoln
3120 Pine Lake Road, Suite R
Lincoln, NE 68516
Phone: 402-328-0120

Omaha # 714
10305 Pacific St.
Omaha, NE 68114
Phone: 402-391-3698

Nevada

Anthem # 280
10345 South Eastern Ave.
Henderson, NV 89052
Phone: 702-407-8673

Carson City # 281
3790 US Highway 395 S,
Suite 401
Carson City, NV 89705
Phone: 775-267-2486

Henderson # 097
2716 North Green Valley
Parkway
Henderson, NV 89014
Phone: 702-433-6773

**Las Vegas
(Decatur Blvd.) # 098**
2101 S. Decatur Blvd.,
Suite 25
Las Vegas, NV 89102
Phone: 702-367-0227

**Las Vegas
(Summerlin) # 086**
7575 West Washington,
Suite 117
Las Vegas, NV 89128
Phone: 702-242-8240

Reno # 082
5035 S. McCarran Blvd.
Reno, NV 89502
Phone: 775-826-1621

New Hampshire

Nashua – Coming Soon!
262 Daniel Webster Hwy
Nashua, NH 03060
Phone: TBD

*Newington (Portsmouth) –
Coming Soon!*
45 Gosling Rd
Newington, NH 03801
Phone: TBD

New Jersey

Edgewater* # 606
715 River Road
Edgewater, NJ 07020
Phone: 201-945-5932

Florham Park* # 604
186 Columbia Turnpike
Florham Park, NJ 07932
Phone: 973-514-1511

Marlton* # 631
300 P Route 73 South
Marlton, NJ 08053
Phone: 856-988-3323

Millburn* # 609
187 Millburn Ave.
Millburn, NJ 07041
Phone: 973-218-0912

Store does not carry alcohol.

Paramus* # 605
404 Rt. 17 North
Paramus, NJ 07652
Phone: 201-265-9624

Princeton # 607
3528 US 1
(Brunswick Pike)
Princeton, NJ 08540
Phone: 609-897-0581

Shrewsbury*
1031 Broad St.
Shrewsbury, NJ 07702
Phone: 732-389-2535

Wayne* # 632
1172 Hamburg Turnpike
Wayne, NJ 07470
Phone: 973-692-0050

Westfield # 601
155 Elm St.
Westfield, NJ 07090
Phone: 908-301-0910

Westwood* # 602
20 Irvington Street
Westwood, NJ 07675
Phone: 201-263-0134

New Mexico

Albuquerque # 166
8928 Holly Ave. NE
Albuquerque, NM 87122
Phone: 505-796-0311

**Albuquerque
(Uptown) # 167**
2200 Uptown Loop NE
Albuquerque, NM 87110
Phone: 505-883-3662

Santa Fe # 165
530 W. Cordova Road
Santa Fe, NM 87505
Phone: 505-995-8145

New York

NY stores sell beer only

Albany – Coming Soon!
79 Wolf Road
Colonie, NY 12205
Phone: TBD

Brooklyn # 558
130 Court St
Brooklyn, NY 11201
Phone: 718-246-8460

Commack # 551
5010 Jericho Turnpike
Commack, NY 11725
Phone: 631-493-9210

Hartsdale # 533
215 North Central Avenue
Hartsdale, NY 10530
Phone: 914-997-1960

Hewlett # 554
1280 West Broadway
Hewlett, NY 11557
Phone: 516-569-7191

Lake Grove # 556
137 Alexander Ave.
Lake Grove, NY 11755
Phone: 631-863-2477

Larchmont # 532
1260 Boston Post Road
Larchmont, NY 10538
Phone: 914-833-9110

Merrick # 553
1714 Merrick Road
Merrick, NY 11566
Phone: 516-771-1012

**New York
(72nd & Broadway) # 542**
2075 Broadway
New York, NY 10023
Phone: 212-799-0028

**New York
(Chelsea) # 543**
675 6th Ave
New York, NY 10010
Phone: 212-255-2106

**New York (Union Square
Grocery) # 540**
142 E. 14th St.
New York, NY 10003
Phone: 212-529-4612

**New York (Union Square
Wine) # 541**
138 E. 14th St.
New York, NY 10003
Phone: 212-529-6326
Alcohol: Wine Only

Oceanside # 552
3418 Long Beach Rd.
Oceanside, NY 11572
Phone: 516-536-9163

Plainview # 555
425 S. Oyster Bay Rd.
Plainview, NY 11803
Phone: 516-933-6900

Queens # 557
90-30 Metropolitan Ave.
Queens, NY 11374
Phone: 718-275-1791

Rochester – Coming Soon!
3349 Monroe Ave
Rochester, NY 14618
Phone: TBD

Scarsdale # 531
727 White Plains Rd.
Scarsdale, NY 10583
Phone: 914-472-2988

Staten Island
2385 Richmond Ave
Staten Island, NY 10314
Phone: 718-370-1085

Westbury – Coming Soon!
900 Old Country Road
Garden City, NY 11530
Phone: TBD

North Carolina

Cary # 741
1393 Kildaire Farms Rd.
Cary, NC 27511
Phone: 919-465-5984

Chapel Hill # 745
1800 E. Franklin St.
Chapel Hill, NC 27514
Phone: 919-918-7871

**Charlotte
(Midtown) # 744**
1133 Metropolitan Ave., Ste. 100
Charlotte, NC 28204
Phone: 704-334-0737

Charlotte (North) # 743
1820 East Arbors Dr.**
(corner of W. Mallard Creek
Church Rd. & Senator Royall Dr.)
Charlotte, NC 28262
Phone: 704-688-9578
[**For accurate driving direc-
tions on the web, please use
1820 W. Mallard Creek
Church Rd.]

Charlotte (South) # 742
6418 Rea Rd.
Charlotte, NC 28277
Phone: 704-543-5249

Raleigh # 746
3000 Wake Forest Rd.
Raleigh, NC 27609
Phone: 919-981-7422

Ohio

Cincinnati # 669
7788 Montgomery Road
Cincinnati, OH 45236
Phone: 513-984-3452

Columbus # 679
3888 Townsfair Way
Columbus, OH 43219
Phone: 614-473-0794

Dublin # 672
6355 Sawmill Road
Dublin, OH 43017
Phone: 614-793-8505

Kettering # 673
328 East Stroop Road
Kettering, OH 45429
Phone: 937-294-5411

Westlake # 677
175 Market Street
Westlake, OH 44145
Phone: 440-250-1592

Woodmere # 676
28809 Chagrin Blvd.
Woodmere, OH 44122
Phone: 216-360-9320

Oregon

Beaverton # 141
11753 S. W. Beaverton
Hillsdale Hwy.
Beaverton, OR 97005
Phone: 503-626-3794

Bend # 150
63455 North
Highway 97, Ste. 4
Bend, OR 97701
Phone: 541-312-4198

Clackamas # 152
9345 SE 82nd Ave (across from
Home Depot)
Happy Valley, OR 97086
Phone: 503-771-6300

Corvallis # 154
1550 NW 9th Street
Corvallis, OR 97330
Phone: 541-753-0048

Eugene # 145
85 Oakway Center
Eugene, OR 97401
Phone: 541-485-1744

Hillsboro # 149
2285 NW 185th Ave.
Hillsboro, OR 97124
Phone: 503-645-8321

Lake Oswego # 142
15391 S. W. Bangy Rd.
Lake Oswego, OR 97035
Phone: 503-639-3238

Medford – Coming Soon!
Northgate Marketplace
1500 Court St.
Medford, OR 97501
Phone: TBD

Portland (SE) # 143
4715 S. E. 39th Avenue
Portland, OR 97202
Phone: 503-777-1601

Portland (NW) # 146
2122 N.W. Glisan
Portland, OR 97210
Phone: 971-544-0788

**Portland
(Hollywood) # 144**
4121 N.E. Halsey St.
Portland, OR 97213
Phone: 503-284-1694

Salem #153
4450 Commercial St.,
Suite 100
Salem, OR 97302
Phone: 503-378-9042

Pennsylvania

Ardmore* # 635
112 Coulter Avenue
Ardmore, PA 19003
Phone: 610-658-0645

Jenkintown* # 633
933 Old York Road
Jenkintown, PA 19046
Phone: 215-885-524

Media* # 637
12 East State Street
Media, PA 19063
Phone: 610-891-2752

North Wales* # 639
1430 Bethlehem Pike
(corner SR 309 & SR 63)
North Wales, PA 19454
Phone: 215-646-5870

Philadelphia* # 634
2121 Market Street
Philadelphia, PA 19103
Phone: 215-569-9282

Pittsburgh* # 638
6343 Penn Ave.
Pittsburgh, PA 15206
Phone: 412-363-5748

Pittsburgh*
1630 Washington Road
Pittsburgh, PA 15228
Phone: 412-835-2212

State College - coming soon!*
1855 North Atherton St.
State College, PA 16803
Phone: TBD

Wayne* # 632
171 East Swedesford Rd.
Wayne, PA 19087
Phone: 610-225-0925

Rhode Island

Warwick* # 518
1000 Bald Hill Rd
Warwick, RI 02886
Phone: 401-821-5368

South Carolina

Columbia – Coming Soon!
4502 Forest Drive
Columbia, SC 29206
Phone: TBD

Greenville
59 Woodruff
Industrial Lane
Greenville, SC 29607
Phone: 864-286-0231

Mt. Pleasant – #752
401 Johnnie Dodds Blvd.
Mt. Pleasant, SC 29464
Phone: 843-884-4037

Tennessee

Knoxville – Coming Soon!
8025 Kingston Pike
Knoxville, TN 37919
Phone: TBD
Alcohol: Beer Only

Nashville # 664
3909 Hillsboro Pike
Nashville, TN 37215
Phone: 615-297-6560
Alcohol: Beer Only

Texas

Austin – Coming Soon!
211 Seaholm Dr, Ste 100
Austin, TX 78703

Dallas (Lower Greenville) – Coming Soon!
2001 Greenville Ave
Dallas, TX 75206

Dallas (Preston Hallow Village) – Coming Soon!
Central Expy & Walnut Hill Ln

Fort Worth
2701 S. Hulen St
For Worth, TX 76107
Phone: 817-922-9107

Houston (Alabama Theater) – Coming Soon!
2922 S Shepherd Dr
Houston, TX 77098

Houston (Memorial Area) – Coming Soon!
1440 S Voss Road
Houston, TX 77057

Plano – Coming Soon!
2400 Preston Rd Ste 200
Plano, TX 75093

San Antonio – Coming Soon!
350 East Basse Rd
San Antonio, TX 78209

The Woodlands
10868 Kuykendahl Road
The Woodlands, TX 77381
Phone: 281-465-0254

Utah

Salt Lake City – Coming Soon!
634 East 400 South
Salt Lake City, UT 84102
Phone: TBD

Virginia

Alexandria # 647
612 N. Saint Asaph Street
Alexandria, VA 22314
Phone: 703-548-0611

Bailey's Crossroads # 644
5847 Leesburg Pike
Bailey's Crossroads,
VA 22041
Phone: 703-379-5883

Centreville # 654
14100 Lee Highway
Centreville, VA 20120
Phone: 703-815-0697

Clarendon
1109 N. Highland St.
Arlington, VA 22201
Phone: 703-351-8015

Fairfax # 643
9464 Main Street
Fairfax, VA 22031
Phone: 703-764-8550

Falls Church # 641
7514 Leesburg Turnpike
Falls Church, VA 22043
Phone: 703-288-0566

Newport News # 656
12551 Jefferson Ave.,
Suite #179
Newport News, VA 23602
Phone: 757-890-0235

Reston # 646
11958 Killingsworth Ave.
Reston, VA 20194
Phone: 703-689-0865

**Richmond
(Short Pump) # 659**
11331 W Broad St, Ste 161
Glen Allen, VA 23060
Phone: 804-360-4098

Springfield # 651
6394 Springfield Plaza
Springfield, VA 22150
Phone: 703-569-9301

Virginia Beach # 660
503 Hilltop Plaza
Virginia Beach, VA 23454
Phone: 757-422-4840

Williamsburg # 657
5000 Settlers Market Blvd (corner of Monticello and Settlers Market)**
Williamsburg, VA 23188
Phone: 757-259-2135
[**For accurate driving directions on the web, please use 5224 Monticello Ave.]

Washington

Ballard # 147
4609 14th Avenue NW
Seattle, WA 98107
Phone: 206-783-0498

Bellevue # 131
15400 N. E. 20th Street
Bellevue, WA 98007
Phone: 425-643-6885

Bellingham # 151
2410 James Street
Bellingham, WA 98225
Phone: 360-734-5166

Burien # 133
15868 1st. Avenue South
Burien, WA 98148
Phone: 206-901-9339

Everett # 139
811 S.E. Everett Mall Way
Everett, WA 98208
Phone: 425-513-2210

Federal Way # 134
1758 S. 320th Street
Federal Way, WA 98003
Phone: 253-529-9242

Issaquah # 138
1495 11th Ave. N.W.
Issaquah, WA 98027
Phone: 425-837-8088

Kirkland # 132
12632 120th Avenue N. E.
Kirkland, WA 98034
Phone: 425-823-1685

Lynnwood # 129
19500 Highway 99,
Suite 100
Lynnwood, WA 98036
Phone: 425-744-1346

Olympia # 156
Olympia West Center
1530 Black Lake Blvd.
Olympia, WA 98502
Phone: 360-352-744

Redmond # 140
15932 Redmond Way
Redmond, WA 98052
Phone: 425-883-1624

Seattle (U. District) # 137
4555 Roosevelt Way NE
Seattle, WA 98105
Phone: 206-547-6299

**Seattle
(Queen Anne Hill) # 135**
112 West Galer St.
Seattle, WA 98119
Phone: 206-378-5536

Seattle (Capitol Hill) # 130
1700 Madison St.
Seattle, WA 98122
Phone: 206-322-7268

Seattle (West)
4545 Fauntleroy Way SW
Seattle, WA 98116
Phone: 206-913-0013

Silverdale
9991 Mickelberry Rd.
Silverdale, WA 98383
Phone: 360-307-7224

Spokane
2975 East 29th Avenue
Spokane, WA 99223
Phone: 509-534-1077

University Place # 148
3800 Bridgeport Way West
University Place, WA 98466
Phone: 253-460-2672

Vancouver # 136
305 SE Chkalov Drive #B1
Vancouver, WA 98683
Phone: 360-883-9000

Wisconsin

Glendale # 711
5600 North Port
Washington Road
Glendale, WI 53217
Phone: 414-962-3382

Madison # 712
1810 Monroe Street
Madison, WI 53711
Phone: 608-257-1916

Although we aim to ensure that the store location information contained here is correct, we will not be responsible for any errors or omissions.